The Family Album

The Family Album

Edited by
ARTHUR AND NANCY DeMOSS

Associate Editor
JOSEPH V. GORMAN

Illustrations by
JOSEPH V. GORMAN

Published by
THE FAMILY ALBUM
Valley Forge

ISBN 0-87981-140-4

LIBRARY OF CONGRESS CATALOG CARD NUMBER 66-21900

PRINTED IN THE UNITED STATES OF AMERICA

ACKNOWLEDGMENTS

Grateful acknowledgment is hereby expressed to all those who have contributed to this book. Any inadvertent omissions of credit will be gladly corrected in future editions.

AMERICAN BAPTIST BOARD OF EDUCATION AND PUBLICATION for "Martin of Tours" by Lillus Mace from *The Secret Place*. Copyright © 1977. Used by permission of the American Baptist Board of Education and Publication.

AMERICAN EDUCATIONAL LEAGUE, Freedom Center, Knotts Berry Farm, for "One United People" by John Jay.

AMERICAN SUNDAY SCHOOL UNION for "Come, O Thou Prince of Peace, etc." by Floyd W. Tomkins from *Prayers For The Quiet Hour* by Floyd W. Tomkins. Copyright © 1926 American Sunday School Union, Philadelphia, Pa.

THE GENERAL COUNCIL OF THE ASSEMBLIES OF GOD for "A Family Is Like a Wheel" by Gwen Weising, reprinted from the Pentecostal Evangel by permission. Copyright © 1977 by The General Council of The Assemblies of God.

THE CHICAGO TRIBUNE for "What Is a Grandparent?" by Joan Beck, used with permission.

CHRISTIAN HERALD for "America's Snowflake Man" by Gloria May Stoddard.

THE CHURCH OF JESUS CHRIST OF LATTER DAY SAINTS for "The Uninvited Dinner Guest" by Geraldine Brook; "Gerald's Secret New Year's Resolutions" by Vicki H. Budge; "Hush" and "Pilgrim Mother Speaks" by Solveig Paulson Russell; "City Robin" and "The Lion And The Mouse" by Frances B. Watts.

COSLETT PUBLISHING COMPANY for "One of the most tragic things, etc." by Dale Carnegie and "A Thing of Beauty Is a Joy Forever" by John Keats from *Young In Heart* by Virginia W. Bass.

DOUBLEDAY AND COMPANY, INC. for "If," Copyright © 1910 by Rudyard Kipling, from *Rudyard Kipling's Verse: Definitive Edition*. Reprinted by permission of Doubleday & Company, Inc., and "Confide In A Friend," author unknown.

FLEMING H. REVELL COMPANY for "Attic Dreams" and "Back Through the Years" by Lucille Crumley from *Thinkables: Meditations For People Who Mean It* by James C. Hefley. Copyright © 1970 by Fleming H. Revell Company. All rights reserved.

FOUNDATION FOR CHRISTIAN LIVING for "The Lone Eagle," excerpted from *A New Birth of Freedom* by Norman Vincent Peale. Copyright ©1973. Used by permission of the Foundation For Christian Living, Pawling, New York 12564.

GOOD NEWS PUBLISHERS for "Can Prayer Save America?"

ACKNOWLEDGMENTS continued on page 176

Contents

Editors' Foreword

In this fourteenth edition of the Family Album we have tried to capture just a few of the many ways in which Christ's love for all of us is revealed.

Each picture, poem, story and Bible passage tells in its own unique way of His presence in art, literature and nature.

We hope this Album brings you the same pleasure we experienced in compiling it. As always, we are delighted to hear from our readers with comments and suggestions. You are the ones to whom this book is dedicated.

Sincerely,

Arthur and Nancy DeMoss
Valley Forge, Pennsylvania

The Family Album

Books are the quietest and most constant of friends; they are the most accessible and wisest of counselors, and the most patient of teachers.
Charles W. Eliot

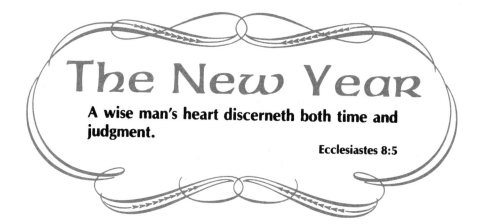

The New Year

A wise man's heart discerneth both time and judgment.

Ecclesiastes 8:5

A Passing Shadow

Only the moon beyond the window-sill—
Only the wind upon a winter hill
Follow the shadow of the dying year,
Watching it fade and swiftly disappear.
Only the pensive share the rendezvous
She keeps with time; her spirit passing
    through
Into remembered ways. Erased from earth,
Only the heart retains her golden worth.

E. Cole Ingle

A Gentle Philosophy

Time is but the stream I go a-fishing in. I drink at it; but while I drink I see the sandy bottom and detect how shallow it is. Its thin current slides away, but eternity remains. I would drink deeper; fish in the sky, whose bottom is pebbly with stars. I cannot count one. I know not the first letter of the alphabet. I have always been regretting that I was not as wise as the day I was born. The intellect is a cleaver; it discerns and rifts its way into the secret of things. I do not wish to be any more busy with my hands than is necessary. My head is hands and feet. I feel all my best faculties concentrated in it. My instinct tells me that my head is an organ for burrowing, as some creatures use their snout and forepaws, and with it I would mine and burrow my way through these hills. I think that the richest vein is somewhere hereabouts; so by the divining rod and thin rising vapors I judge; and here I will begin to mine.

Henry David Thoreau

January First

Here I stand, Lord
Looking puzzled
Holding a pad of stubs in my hand.
Where did all the tickets go?
All 365 of them
So quickly—

Thank you for the new book
All ready to be used.
I'll treasure each ticket
And use them
Gratefully,
Hopefully, for YOU!

Violet Munro

A New Year Prayer

Merciful Father, Lord of all,
Who marks the tiny sparrow's fall,
Allow Thy gentle healing grace
To calm the tumult of our race.
God guard and guide our nation's head,
Allow him ever to be led
By principles of highest worth.
Let this great nation of our birth
Lean wholly, Lord, upon Thy will,
And blest with peace be grateful still.

Forgive, where stumbling we are wrong;
Fill saddened hearts with happy song;
Give strength where faith is weak and low;
Let love like Thine our lives o'erflow.

We thank Thee for Thy presence near,
For blessings granted the past year;
Lord guard us, guide us as we tread
The New Year paths that lie ahead.

Geraldine Fay Gray

GOLDEN THOUGHTS

Moments are like uncut diamonds. Discard them and their value will never be known; improve them and they will become the brightest gems in a useful life.

Ralph Waldo Emerson

I need a thousand years to do what I have in mind.

Victor Hugo

You may delay, but Time will not.

Benjamin Franklin

A moment's insight is sometimes worth a life's experience.

Oliver Wendell Holmes

The Mystery Of Time

That great mystery of Time, were there no other; the illimitable, silent never-resting thing called Time, rolling, rushing on, swift, silent, like an all-embracing ocean tide, on which we and all the Universe swim like exhalations, like apparitions which are, and then are not: this is forever very literally a miracle; a thing to strike us dumb—for we have no word to speak about it!

Carlyle

A New Year Brings A New Beginning

As the New Year starts
    and the old year ends
There's no better time
    to make amends
For all the things
    we sincerely regret
And wish in our hearts
    we could somehow forget—
We all make mistakes,
    for it's human to err,
But no one need ever
    give up in despair,
For God gives us all
    a brand-new beginning,
A chance to start over
    and repent of our sinning—
And when God forgives us
    we too must forgive
And resolve to do better
    each day that we live
By constantly trying
    to be like Him more nearly
And to trust in His wisdom
    and love Him more dearly—
Assured that we're never
    out of His care
And we're always welcome
    to seek Him in prayer.

Helen Steiner Rice

America's Snowflake Man

Few natural wonders evoke as much awe of God's craftsmanship as snowflakes. Each unique pattern testifies to the abundance of God's creative powers.

Yet the beauty we now take for granted remained unknown less than a century ago. Wilson A. Bentley, of Jericho, Vermont, unlocked their secrets. Spurred by his wonder at God's creation, he spent 50 years studying snow.

Willie Bentley first peered at snowflakes through an old microscope when he was 15 years old. Though his parents' farmhouse offered few luxuries, his mother gave him a microscope she had used in her earlier schoolteaching days. Few people then knew what a snowflake looked like close-up, so Willie's wonder was roused by a verse he read in the family Bible: "Hast thou entered into the treasures of the snow? or hast thou seen the treasures of the hail?" *(Job 38:22)*. The magnified snow crystals amazed him. Each one was a glittering masterpiece created by the Great Designer. He observed to his mother, "Each snowflake is as different from its fellows as we human beings are from our fellows."

Determined to preserve their beauty, Willie observed and drew 300 snowflakes during the next three winters. He was unable to copy their designs accurately because they melted so fast. His father, a practical man, tried to discourage the time-consuming hobby. But Willie dreamed of using a special camera which could make photographs through an attached microscope. When his parents gave him such a camera on his 17th birthday, he felt confident he could finally succeed. His persistence paid off after three more years of experiments. On January 15, 1885, he produced the first successful photomicrograph of a snow crystal.

To counteract his five-foot height, he had to invent pulleys and levers for his extensive camera. He worked outside for hours in temperatures of 25 to 0 degrees F. The Bentley farm had no indoor plumbing, so he washed his prints in a pasture spring. Despite these hardships, he discovered how to reproduce white snowflake images onto a black background so that each detail was visible.

As a result of his experiments, Bentley made hundreds of beautiful snowflake prints. Sometimes he clustered and photographed several prints together. One of these, a print of snowflakes in the form of a cross, sat on his often-played piano beside a hymnal. His collection of photomicrographs of unique snowflakes, which peaked at 5,831, testified to the extent of God's creativity.

The public finally saw Bentley's work when he co-authored an article on snowflakes with Vermont's state geologist. The article appeared in Appleton's Popular Scientific Monthly in 1898. He was soon recognized as the world's foremost authority on snowflakes, and christened "The Snowflake Man." Professors, artists, jewelers, and silk and glass manufacturers bought his prints. Some of them were used to design stained glass windows for a Jewish temple in Tulsa. He was invited to speak at scientific gatherings, universities, churches and clubs in Canada and New England.

Despite his fame, Bentley never became rich. He sold each of his prints for the cost of the materials—about five cents. He used income from his lectures to buy additional materials.

"I am a poor man," he once said, "except for the satisfaction I get out of my work. In that respect I am the richest man in the world. I wouldn't change places with a king. I have my snowflakes.

"The greatest charm which this unique study possesses is that these treasures are absolutely inexhaustible. For all time this annual miracle of the snows will recur."

In 1924, the American Meteorological Society awarded Bentley its first research grant for his "forty years of extremely patient work." The world shared the final fruits of this labor after the United States Weather Bureau raised additional money so that Bentley could prepare a book of 2,453 photos of frost, dew and snowflakes.

Two days before Christmas, 1931, Willie Bentley died of pneumonia in the farmhouse where he had been born 66 years before. Today, a bronze plaque in the village of Jericho Corners pays tribute to this remarkable farmer and scientist who for half a century served God and man by preserving the beauty of snowflakes.

Gloria May Stoddard

Time

Tentative time
On timid feet
Pussy-footed to my door
Filtered through the key-hole
Crept across the floor
Rubbed against my ankle
Leaped upon my lap
And ensnared me gently
In her purring trap.

A. V. Riasanovsky

Winter White

Softly, silently, the snowflakes fall,
And flannel-posted fences raise their heads
Along the winding miles of ermine shrubs,
Down roadsides lined with crystal flower beds.
The intricate design of frosted lakes
Gleams dully 'neath a matted sky of grey,
Pale pointed fingers of the north wind tear
The frozen branches roughly from its way.
Like a scene within a water globe,
The smallest hand need only shake to see
The dazzling swirl that breathlessly descends,
To shape and shade in fragile mystery . . .
So the world appears to me tonight,
Dressed in flowing robes of WINTER WHITE!

Grace E. Easley

What Is Time?

What is time? The shadow on the dial, the striking of the clock, the running of the sand day and night, summer and winter, months, years, centuries—these are but arbitrary and outward signs, the measure of Time, not Time itself. Time is the life of the soul.

Henry Wadsworth Longfellow

Let's Read It Together
the children's corner

Gerald's Secret New Year's Resolutions

Gerald woke up on New Year's Day feeling tired.

"Time to get up," called Mother. "Breakfast is on the table."

When Gerald came into the kitchen rubbing his eyes, Mother asked, "Did you make any New Year's resolutions?"

Gerald didn't answer his mother's question just then. He felt like complaining that he hadn't had enough sleep, but instead he forced a smile and said, "Morning, Mom." Then Gerald saw that they were having oatmeal for breakfast. He was going to say, "Ugh! I can't stand oatmeal." Instead he said, "Thanks, Mom, you're sure nice to have my breakfast ready."

"Good morning, Gerald," said Dad. "Greg and Jennie and I have been talking about our New Year's resolutions."

Greg and Jennie were Gerald's little brother and sister. They were twins and it seemed to Gerald that all they ever did was argue.

"I resolved to eat all of my oatmeal every morning," said Jennie with a giggle.

"Big deal!" said Greg. "That's no resolution. You love oatmeal."

"Jennie also resolved to make her bed every morning before playing," said Dad. "And Greg resolved to write a letter to Grandma and Grandpa once a week and make his bed every morning."

"How about you, Gerald?" asked his mother again. "Have you made any resolutions?"

"As a matter of fact, I have," answered Gerald with a grin. "But they're a secret."

"A secret!" cried Greg. "That's no fun! How will we know if you're keeping your resolutions?"

"Oh, you'll know," answered Gerald with an even bigger grin. "I made five resolutions and you're supposed to guess what they are by watching me."

"Ah ha!" said Mom. "That explains a few things that have already surprised me this morning. I think I know what two of your resolutions are."

"Well, one of *my* resolutions is to see that the garage stays clean,"

Continued on page 16

Continued from page 15

said Dad. "And I notice that someone has left my tools scattered all over the workbench. I expect that *someone* to put them back where they belong."

"I didn't touch them," said Jennie.

"I haven't been in the garage," Greg declared.

"I didn't do it," was what Gerald was about to say, but then he remembered using them. "I used them, Dad, and I'll put them away today for sure," he promised.

Dad smiled. "I think I'm beginning to guess one of your secret resolutions, too," he said, winking at Gerald.

"What is it?" teased Jennie.

"You have to guess," Gerald answered.

"I'm going to tidy up the garage this morning," Dad announced. "Why don't each of you do whatever you need to, and then we'll play a game of football when I'm through."

"I'll make my bed," shouted Jennie and Greg at the same time, and they both ran off to their bedrooms.

"I'll do these dishes," Mom said and began clearing the table.

"I'll warm up the football," Gerald almost said; then he remembered. "Can I help you, Mom, before I put away the tools?"

After Gerald finished helping with the dishes and putting away Dad's tools, he went to his room to make his bed and get the football. When he walked down the hall he found Jennie and Greg arguing over who should put away an animal game that was spread on the hall floor.

"You got it out," complained Jennie.

"You helped me play with it," said Greg.

"Will you two ever quit fighting?" was what Gerald nearly said, but he didn't.

"Hey, you two, it will just take a minute to put this game away if you both help. In fact, I'll help you. Let's see how fast we can pick it up."

Gerald's family had fun playing football and doing many other things that day. By evening Gerald's family thought they had guessed all five of his resolutions. They wrote them down and gave them to Gerald to see if they had guessed right.

And they had!

Can you guess what Gerald promised to be when he made his New Year's resolutions? Unscramble these five words if you don't already know: rfeeluhc, loteip, lufhtrut, plufelh, gmakceepain

Answer:

cheerful, polite, truthful, helpful, peacemaking

Vicki H. Budge

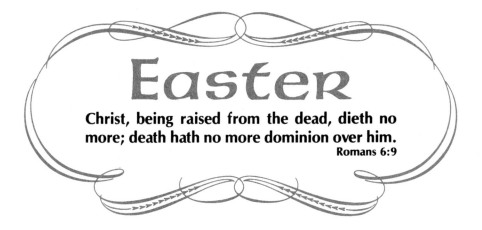

Easter

Christ, being raised from the dead, dieth no more; death hath no more dominion over him.
Romans 6:9

Love, Joy, Peace...

"But the fruit of the Spirit is love, joy, peace, longsuffering,
gentleness, goodness, faith, meekness, temperance:
against such there is no law" (Galatians 5:22.23).

Jesus said,
"I am the vine, ye are the branches: He that
abideth in me, and I in him, the same bringeth forth
much fruit: for without me ye can do nothing"
(John 15:5).

I searched this world for love
That I might be happy and secure.

In all my wanderings I found
Only the world's sadness and confusion.

I searched this world for joy
That I might know laughter and lightheartedness.

In all my wanderings I found
Only the world's tears and heaviness.

I searched this world for peace
That I might know contentment and rest.

In all my wanderings I found
Only the world's discord and turmoil.

Continued on page 20

Continued from page 19

In desperation I cried,
"There is no lasting love or joy or peace!"

Then I was pointed to a lonely hill and a lonely cross.
And suddenly my eyes were opened.

I saw God's Son and the cruelty of Calvary.
"Too great a price!" I groaned.

For there, for the first time, I saw genuine love,
As Jesus uttered in anguish, "Father forgive them."

I saw true joy, that One so sinless
Could endure that cross "for the joy that was set before him."

"It is finished," He said.
And I saw deep peace.

I found love in giving,
   joy in doing the will of the Father,
and peace in the finished work of Calvary.

   Then I knelt and cried.
      "Dear Jesus, your blood was shed for me;
      Cleanse me and redeem me."

Ruth S. Tomszak

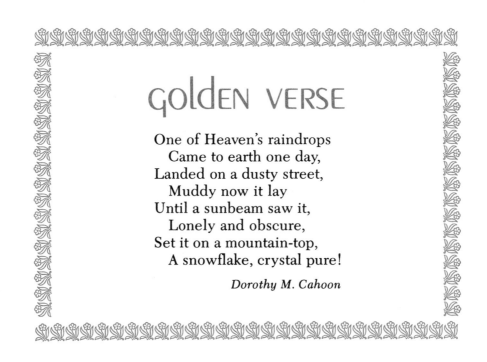

GOLDEN VERSE

One of Heaven's raindrops
   Came to earth one day,
Landed on a dusty street,
   Muddy now it lay
Until a sunbeam saw it,
   Lonely and obscure,
Set it on a mountain-top,
   A snowflake, crystal pure!

Dorothy M. Cahoon

A Prayer In Spring

Oh, give us pleasure in the flowers today;
And give us not to think so far away
As the uncertain harvest; keep us here
All simply in the springing of the year.

Oh, give us pleasure in the orchard white,
Like nothing else by day, like ghosts by night;
And make us happy in the happy bees,
The swarm dilating round the perfect trees.

And make us happy in the darting bird
That suddenly above the bees is heard,
The meteor that thrusts in with needle bill,
And off a blossom in mid air stands still.

For this is love and nothing else is love,
The which it is reserved for God above
To sanctify to what far ends He will,
But which it only needs that we fulfil.

Robert Frost

The Dawn Of Hope

There were citizens from many countries in Singapore the day it fell to the Japanese back in 1942. I was Canadian, working for the Red Cross. Civilians were rounded up, 4,266 of us and herded into Changi jail that had been built for 450 prisoners. We were to be there, those of us who lived that long, until the war's end nearly four years later.

By day we jostled each other in the dank, high-walled yard of the women's section. At night we slept three to a cubicle that was seven feet long, a little over six and a half feet wide. We were fed soup made from a sort of coarse spinach. It was all we had to eat unless you knew how to catch the rats.

Crowding and hunger, flies and filth—these were obvious conditions. Yet there was another one, invisible but perhaps the most frightening of all: a sense of utter isolation. We were permitted no news of families and home; sometimes it seemed that even God had drawn far off.

As that first Easter approached, our longing to see a sign that God had not forgotten us grew desperate. For many of us, Easter meant a sunrise service. Here was one thing that had not changed: the sun still rose each morning until it broke even over the top of those high walls. What if, Easter morning, we could but stand together in the courtyard, and as the sun rose, sing hymns of praise and hope!

But the idea had to be presented to the prison commandant. Because I still had my Red Cross armband, I put it on and went to see him. We hoped I might appear as an "official" to the status-conscious Japanese.

The commandant sat at a desk. I made our brief plea.

"Why?" he said.

"Because—because Christ rose from the dead on Easter morning."

I could see suspicion in his eyes.

"No. Return to the compound."

I bowed, backed away and bowed again in the elaborate Oriental ceremony of leave-taking. I had been in the East long enough to know that he would not refuse a request for a return visit while I was still his "guest." So at the door I asked and received permission to return.

This strange little drama of "request and refusal" was repeated twelve separate times.

At last, early in April, permission was granted to the women's compound: "Women prisoners may sing for five minutes in court-yard number one, Changi jail, at dawn on Easter morning."

We were galvanized into activity. We chose a hymn and a choir leader, rehearsed, assigned positions, timed everything. When you have nothing to do all day long, very little will occupy a great deal of time.

The news—for everything is news in the vacuum of a POW camp—raced through the men's section. Some of their cells over-looked courtyard number one and they lavished days on planning a quota system: so many seconds at a window for each man so that as many as possible could watch on Easter morning.

At last the day came. We were up before dawn and formed in our processional. Humming softly we filed into the courtyard. Only one guard was there—the first guard we had ever seen without a gun. We took our positions, waiting in the chill, grey dawn, silent, thankful Christ had risen. Our choir leader raised her make-shift baton:

> *Low in the grave He lay*
> *Jesus, my Saviour,*
> *Waiting the coming day . . .*
> *He arose a victor*
> *From that dark domain . . .*
> *Hallelujah, Christ arose!*

Sunlight burst over the wall. We held our breaths, expectant, believing, ready for a miracle.

But it was over. Over so soon. Silently we marched back—then the miracle happened.

As I reached the passageway the guard stepped up, reached inside his brown shirt and drew out one of the little flowers (no bigger than a snap dragon) that grow in such profusion in Malaya—a tiny orchid. Placing it in my hand the guard spoke so low I had to bend close to hear.

"Christ *did* rise," he said. Then a smart military about-face and he was gone down the passageway.

I stood where he left me, eyes brimming with tears, knowing that we could never again feel forsaken in Changi jail.

No one will ever tell me that that tiny orchid was an ordinary flower. It rooted itself to a little piece of bark and bloomed and budded all the years of our imprisonment. Passed from hand to hand, it was evidence of God's beauty when all around us was man's ugliness. We knew that our Easter hymn had not been a lonely cry in the wilderness, but rather part of a swelling chorus all over the earth, singing out in the night of hate that the sunrise of His love would surely come.

Ethel Rogers Mulvany

Fasting And Feasting

LENT SHOULD be more than a time of fasting.

It should also be a joyous season of feasting. Lent is a time to fast *from* certain things and to feast *on* others. It is a season in which we should:

Fast from judging others; feast on the Christ indwelling them.
Fast from emphasis on differences; feast on the unity of all life.
Fast from apparent darkness; feast on the reality of light.
Fast from thoughts of illness; feast on the healing power of God.

Fast from words that pollute; feast on phrases that purify.
Fast from discontent; feast on gratitude.
Fast from anger; feast on patience.
Fast from pessimism; feast on optimism.

Fast from worry; feast on divine order.
Fast from complaining; feast on appreciation.
Fast from negatives; feast on affirmatives.
Fast from unrelenting pressures; feast on unceasing prayer.

Fast from hostility; feast on nonresistance.
Fast from bitterness; feast on forgiveness.
Fast from self-concern; feast on compassion for others.
Fast from personal anxiety; feast on eternal Truth.

Fast from discouragement; feast on hope.
Fast from facts that depress; feast on verities that uplift.
Fast from lethargy; feast on enthusiams.
Fast from suspicion; feast on truth.

Fast from thoughts that weaken; feast on promises that inspire.
Fast from shadows of sorrow; feast on the sunlight of serenity.
Fast from idle gossip; feast on purposeful silence.
Fast from problems that overwhelm; feast on prayer
    that undergirds.

William Arthur Ward

His Tears Upon The Rocks

Bow your head low, once-proud, once holy city
For out of your teeming streets, reeking with wickedness
He walked His weary way, and climbed a hill to find a place apart,
To kneel beneath the olive trees and mourn . . .
To know the lonely feeling of rejection
By His own, whom He so loved, but who received Him not!
Once, a few short days ago, you welcomed Him.
(Your thunderous "Hosannah's" still ringing in His ears.)
Alone now, and utterly forgotten in agony of loneliness, He hears
The jeering of the rabble, mocking as the thunder
Echoing through the hills. And here He spills
His life's blood, wrung from Him in agonizing sweat. And yet . . .
The olive trees now witness His forgiving words for thee,
The night His tears upon the rocks spilled out in agony!

Flora Allison Hagglund

I Wept With Mary

I wept with Mary as she knelt
Bereaved and clinging to His cross.
I wept when she kissed His feet
Heart torn, by her mother's loss.

She received Him to this world;
Knelt, clinging there when He died.
And through all His earthly days
For her faithful love, I cried.

In this black crucifixion hour
When all twelve friends had fled;
Mary climbed Golgotha's Hill
And weeping stood—her Child was dead.

Lucille Crumley

Conversation On Calvary

Oh Cross on which our blessed Saviour died,
Do you bemoan the fates that fashioned you
From tree to cross, where He was crucified,
And would you, if you could, begin anew?

Can you recall when you were young and green,
A stalwart sapling straining towards the light,
So glad to be part of the forest scene
And never dreaming of your present plight?

A master carpenter, He loved fine wood
And He created many works of art
For people far and near. Cross, if you could,
Would you not rather be a chair, a cart?

Oh Cross! If I were you my life would seem
The essence of a nightmare's cruelest theme!

Ah Christian! Could I but forget! But yes,
My years of growth, the sun and warming rain,
The gentle breeze that stirred my leafy dress,
These I remember plus the haunting pain.

When I was felled my grief became complete,
For when He bore me up to Calvary
I suffered too. When sharp nails pierced His feet
And then He bled, I shared His agony.

How many trees were felled the same as I;
But they adorn some home or fill a need,
A dream? Why could not I, too, beautify
Or aid in mankind's progress, not impede?

Oh Christian! Could I have but one desire,
Let fate decree I light some poor man's fire!

Gladys M. Seiders

Where Were They?

Where were they when the Master wept
There in the garden all alone?
Where were they when the crowds drew near,
Hurling bitter word and stone?
Where were they when His back was scourged
There in the courtyard publicly?
Where were they when His head bowed low,
And He hung from a Cross on Calvary?

Where were they when the lots were cast,
For the last of His few and simple clothes?
Where were they when His side was pierced,
And the skies grew dark and the dead arose?
"LONG BEFORE MY TIME" you say,
Speaking the words so easily,
But the lonely weep . . . and the poor reach out,
. . . AND WHERE ARE WE????

Grace E. Easley

Good Friday

"Even unto death My soul is sad,
Can you not wait up with Me through this?
Peter, thou shalt soon deny Me thrice,
Judas shall betray Me with a kiss!
Pilate shall appear before the crowd
And wash his hands that never shall be clean,
Three crosses shall be raised on Golgotha,
And Mine shall be the one that's in between.
Hanging thus between the earth and sky,
Shall My side be opened with a spear,
Born to die that sin may be no more,
For this alone, what was permitted here!"
How shameful, Lord, that NOW as even THEN,
. . . FOOLS MAY WALK THE EARTH DISGUISED AS MEN!

Grace E. Easley

March Magic

Against the lowering dismal skies
The maple shakes her shaggy locks
    and stands aghast,
      bared arms akimbo in the cutting wind,
And windowpanes are streaked
    with sudden tears,
While autumn's leaves, like impish brownies, swirl,
    leap, and cavort in frenzied dance.

Now comes the sun, and slashing
    through the gloom
It brightens woodland paths
    with sudden fire
    and sets the treetops blazing
    in its wake.
The rain-tears check their racing flight
    down glassy cheeks
And halt in frozen, rounded crystal drops
    to watch the fleeing whitecaps
    roll across the gray.
From brilliant splashing gypsy shades
    the western sky fades into deepening dusk,
The wind mounts high and ruffles
    scattered clouds;
A husky Hercules, it whistles shrilly,
    like a rowdy at the timid dark.
So March, that artful showman,
    gives a varied pageantry
    of sun and shower, of warmth and chill;
She runs the gamut from deep snowbanks
    piled along the creek
To violets gay and robin's cheerful trill.
And then, to add the climax to her show,
Tossed from her hat, a mad March hare
    goes skipping down the lane!

Ruby A. Jones

I Planted A Rose

I planted a rose and I talked with God
I looked straight into the high, bright blue
And I said, "Dear God, you do the rest,
I have done all that I can do."

The sun shone warm on the moist brown earth,
The wind from the south cooled my lifted face,
And I think God came from the far blue sky
To watch in my small sweet garden space.

For this morning I found it, the lovely thing:
A pink rose proud on its red-thorned stem,
And there, like little bright candles lit,
Were the pink-tipped buds, a score of them.

I believe God comes for a little while
When any new flower takes root and grows,
And I am quite sure that He comes and stays
When a woman prays as she plants a rose.

Grace Noll Crowell

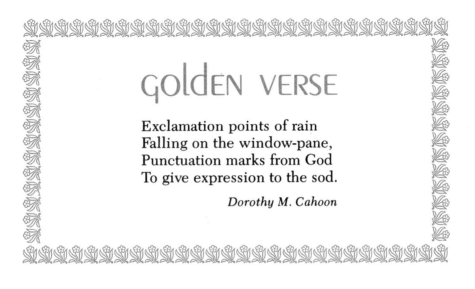

GOLDEN VERSE

Exclamation points of rain
Falling on the window-pane,
Punctuation marks from God
To give expression to the sod.

Dorothy M. Cahoon

The Mountain In Spring

The mountain no longer needs her soft white
    coat with glistening fringe of trees
      against the morning sky.
She has discarded her somber dress of gray
    for new-life green
      splashed with darker evergreen,
        dogwood and redbud,
      trimmed with ribbons of clear mountain streams
        sparkling in the sunlight.
In the early morning her cape of dew is
    set with diamonds.
Beneath her, budding trees are dancing patterns
    of sun and shade
      among wild iris, violets and sweet williams
      at her feet.
Birds without number sing God's praises
    for such beauty.

Leota Campbell

The Rhodora

In May, when sea-winds pierced our solitudes,
I found the fresh Rhodora in the woods,
Spreading its leafless blooms in a damp nook,
To please the desert and the sluggish brook.
The purple petals, fallen in the pool,
Made the black water with their beauty gay;
Here might the redbird come his plumes to cool,
And court the flower that cheapens his array.

Rhodora! if the sages ask thee why
This charm is wasted on the earth and sky,
Tell them, dear, that if eyes were made for seeing,
Then Beauty is its own excuse for being:
Why thou were there, O rival of the rose!
I never thought to ask, I never knew:
But, in my simple ignorance, suppose
The self-same Power that brought me there brought you.

Ralph Waldo Emerson

Spring Grass

Spring grass, there is a dance to be danced for you.
Come up, spring grass, if only for young feet.
Come up, spring grass, young feet ask you.

Smell of the young spring grass,
You're a mascot riding on the wind horses.
You came to my nose and spiffed me. This is your lucky year.

Young spring grass just after the winter,
Shoots of the big green whisper of the year,
Come up, if only for young feet.
Come up, young feet ask you.

Carl Sandburg

The Planting Of The Apple Tree

What plant we in this apple tree?
Buds, which the breath of summer days
Shall lengthen into leafy sprays;
Boughs where the thrush, with crimson breast,
Shall haunt, and sing, and hide her nest;
We plant, upon the sunny lea,
A shadow for the noontide hour,
A shelter from the summer shower,
When we plant the apple tree.

What plant we in this apple tree?
Fruits that shall swell in sunny June,
And redden in the August noon,
And drop, when gentle airs come by,
That fan the blue September sky,
While children come, with cries of glee,
And seek them where the fragrant grass
Betrays their bed to those who pass,
At the foot of the apple tree.

William Cullen Bryant

Jesus Rises From The Dead

As the day began to dawn, Mary, Jesus' mother, Mary Magdalene and some other women of Galilee were already awake and gathering spices to take to Jesus' tomb.

It was still dark and the streets of the city were deserted as the women started toward the garden where Jesus was buried. But they knew, by the time they reached the tomb, there would be enough light to see to anoint Jesus' body with the spices they had gathered.

But the women were concerned about one thing. A huge stone sealed the tomb and they weren't strong enough to roll it away.

The sun was up as the women came into the garden. Suddenly they stopped. "Look!" one of them cried. "The stone has already been moved! How can this be?"

They ran to the tomb, then suddenly stopped. They couldn't believe what they saw. Directly in front of them, sitting on a rock, was a creature whose face was as bright as lightning and whose garments were as white as snow.

"It's an angel!" one of the women said.

The rest of them turned to run away, but the angel called to them.

"Fear not," the angel said. "I know you are looking for Jesus. He is not here. He has risen, as He said He would. Come, I will show you where Jesus lay before He rose from the dead."

The women cautiously entered the tomb and saw the place where Jesus' body had been.

But the tomb was empty, except for another angel who sat beside the place where Jesus' body had been placed on Friday afternoon.

The second angel told the women, "Go and tell the disciples that Jesus has gone to the mountain in Galilee where he told them He would go. Go and you will see Him there."

They ran from the tomb to find Peter and the disciples. The disciples were afraid since Jesus died, and were hiding. When they finally found the disciples, the women were trembling with excitement. They told the men all the amazing things they had heard and seen at the tomb.

The disciples did not believe them. They had all been under a terrible strain since Jesus was taken and crucified. They thought Jesus' death had been too upsetting for the women. They thought they were beginning to imagine things.

"But we were there!" the women said. "We saw the empty tomb! And one of the angels said to tell Peter that Jesus would go to Galilee."

"Then we should go and see for ourselves," said John. "We should not be waiting here."

Peter agreed, but the other disciples still did not believe the women. They decided not to go to the tomb.

But Peter and John wanted to know if the women were telling the truth. They ran all the way to the garden with Mary Magdalene trying to keep up with them.

John arrived at the tomb first and looked inside. The linen shroud that Jesus had been wrapped in was the only thing there. Jesus and the angels were gone.

When Peter, who was older than John, finally got to the tomb, he went right in to look around. He was amazed. The linens which had covered Jesus' body were neatly folded. They knew a thief wouldn't take the time to do this, but who else would take the body away? They were both puzzled.

As they started slowly back toward the city, they passed Mary Magdalene on her way to the tomb. They told her what they had seen—just an empty tomb. They had seen no angels. They had not seen Jesus' body. Just the linen cloth and nothing else. But they still didn't believe He rose from the dead. They would have to have other signs to be convinced.

Mary Magdalene continued on her way to the tomb. Peter and John were probably right, she thought. Thieves must have stolen Jesus' body. She shouldn't have allowed her hopes to get so high.

She leaned against the entrance to the tomb and cried. Her Master was dead and His body had been stolen. She felt terrible.

Suddenly she heard voices coming from inside the tomb. She was afraid but she looked inside. The two angels were there! She hadn't imagined the whole thing! The angels were real! How had Peter and John missed them?

"Why are you crying?" the angels asked.

Perhaps the angels could help her, Mary thought. She had to tell her troubles to someone.

"Because someone has taken my Master away, and I don't know where they have taken Him," she answered.

Just then she heard footsteps on the path outside the tomb and she turned to see who was there. The sun was shining into her eyes, and she couldn't see who it was. Mary thought He was the caretaker of the garden. He would certainly know what happened to Jesus' body.

Continued on page 34

Continued from page 33

"Why are you crying?" He asked. "Are you looking for someone?"

Mary was startled when the Man spoke. His voice sounded very familiar.

"Oh, please, sir," she pleaded. "If you have taken Jesus away, please tell me where He is now."

The Man said only one word—"Mary."

He didn't have to say anything else. She knew who the Man was. It was her Lord and Master, Jesus Christ. He was alive! He had risen from the dead as He said he would.

Mary was overcome with joy. She fell to her knees and hugged Him to her. She would never let Him go.

"You cannot keep Me here, Mary," Jesus said. "I have to go to My Father to be with Him in Heaven.

"Go tell my brothers that I will meet them in Galilee."

Mary, her heart beating with joy, ran from the garden to tell the disciples. Jesus was alive! He had risen from the dead! She had seen Him and the disciples would soon see Him, too.

She told them to go to the mountain in Galilee. They went up to the mountain and Jesus came to them. And when they saw Him, they had no more doubts. They all knelt down and worshipped Him.

Room To Spare

A bumblebee,
A butterfly,
The rain came down,
They didn't know why.

But under a toadstool,
It isn't the same,
They share togetherness
And no more rain.

Edith Mize

Home and Family

Come home with me, and refresh thyself, and I will give thee a reward.

I Kings 13:7

A Family Is Like A Wheel

While walking through a Montana woods one day, I came upon the remains of an old, horse-drawn wagon. The slivered wood of the body rested on the ground. Pieces of iron lay scattered about.

Most of the wheels were off, and the various parts were strewn about; but one wheel remained intact, held together by the iron rim.

I sat looking at the decaying wagon, thinking about the family that had once ridden to the nearest town—15 or 20 miles away. I wondered what they were like. Was it a large family? Most were in those days.

Was the father a quiet man or a rough, boisterous miner? Was the mother a warm, tender person or a scolding, nagging shrew? I could only guess what that family had been like.

But as I sat staring at the wheel, I began to think.

A family is like a wheel. That old wheel would have come apart years ago except for the strong band of iron that encircled and held it together. The father is the rim of the family. He cushions the bumps and blows the family must take.

It's the father who protects and keeps all the other parts bound tightly together. It's he who meets the outside world, grinding against it, even as the rim grinds against the ground.

It's his strong love, made even stronger by knowing the love of God, that encircles the family, holding the members closely together.

At the center of the wheel is the hub around which the whole wheel turns. A mother is like the hub. She centers the family.

It's her function to keep things moving smoothly. She mends bruised knees, torn dresses, and broken hearts. She dries dishes

Continued on page 38

Continued from page 37

and tear-stained faces. She prays for grace, courage, wisdom, and patience. She plans, promotes, encourages, corrects, listens, and learns.

The children are the spokes of the wheel. They may be many or few. Spokes must be firmly attached to both the hub and the rim if the wheel is to go anywhere.

Broken spokes may indicate too much uncushioned stress. The spokes may get loosened from either the hub or the rim and fall out. Some are broken off by a foreign object that catches between them.

Children too may become loosened from the influence of their parents and fall prey to influences outside the home. The father's role of interpreting the world to his children becomes doubly important in times of great stress. Prayerful, considerate guidance from parents keeps the children tightly locked into place in the family unit.

Wheels are vital to this nation's economy. Industry, travel, and other aspects of American life turn on wheels.

Without wheels this nation can go nowhere. Think of them; airplane wheels, automobile wheels, train wheels, and bicycle wheels; wheels in machines, wheelbarrows, wheelchairs, and wheels of computer tape; potters' wheels, steering wheels, tractor wheels, and timing gears. Yes, wheels are vital to the American way of life.

But even more vital to this great land are strong families. Families should be tight units like wheels, all parts working for a common purpose. Imagine a wheel in which the hub wanted to go one direction, the rim another, and the spokes were left to fly in all directions! That's a graphic description of many American families where each member is determined to do his own thing and go his own way. Without strong families united in love and direction our country will suffer.

It is not the wheel that determines the direction it will go; it is some superior source. For the American family the wisest choice is to become firmly locked into God through Jesus Christ His Son.

Lack of energy may someday stop or slow the wheels of this nation, but with God there will never be an energy shortage. His power is eternal. By His power your family can keep moving together as an undivided unit toward an eternal goal called heaven.

Gwen Weising

What Sort Of A Father Are You?

What sort of a father are you to your boy?
  Do you know if your standing is good?
Do you ever take stock of yourself and check up
  Your accounts with your boy as you should?

Do you ever reflect on your conduct with him?
  Are you all that a father should be?
Do you send him away when you're anxious to read
  Or let him climb up on your knee?

Have you time to bestow on the boy when he comes
  With his questions—to tell him the truth?
Or do you neglect him, and leave him alone
  To work out the problems of youth?

Do you ever go walking with him, hand in hand?
  Do you plan little outings for him?
Does he ever look forward to camping with you?
  Or are you eternally grim?

Come, father, reflect! Does he know you today?
  And do you know him as you should?
Is gold so important to you that you leave
  It to chance that your boy will be good?

Take stock of yourself and consider the lad,
  Your time and your thoughts are his due.
How would you answer your God should He ask
  What sort of a father are you?

Author Unknown

GOLDEN SCRIPTURE

At the same time, saith the Lord, will I be the God of all the families of Israel, and they shall be my people.

Jeremiah 31:1

Family Album Favorite

Little Boy Blue

The little toy dog is covered with dust,
But sturdy and staunch he stands;
The little toy soldier is red with rust,
And his musket molds in his hands.

Time was when the little toy dog was new,
And the soldier was passing fair;
And that was the time when our Little Boy Blue
Kissed them and put them there.

"Now don't you go till I come," he said,
"And don't you make any noise!"
So, toddling off to his trundle bed,
He dreamt of the pretty toys;

And, as he was dreaming, an angel song
Awakened our Little Boy Blue—
Oh! the years are many, the years are long,
But the little toy friends are true!

Ay, faithful to Little Boy Blue they stand,
Each in the same old place,
Awaiting the touch of a little hand
The smile of a little face;

And they wonder, as waiting the long years through
In the dust of that little chair,
What has become of our Little Boy Blue,
Since he kissed them and put them there.

Eugene Field

What Is A Grandparent?

One of the happiest dimensions of a small child's life is usually his grandparents, because . . .

A grandfather is an extra dime or quarter whenever you need one, without saying, "What did you do with that money I gave you last Saturday?"

A grandmother is sugar cookies and chocolate chip cookies and peanut butter cookies and not counting how many you eat and not always noticing how close it is to dinnertime.

A grandfather is for telling you secret stories about when your father was little and how he got a spanking.

A grandfather is for saying, "Of course he needs a watch, a fine boy like that—why, he's almost eight years old."

A grandmother is a soft lap on a rocking chair who doesn't put you down and go away to take care of your little sister just because she's crying.

Grandparents are to keep the baby so you and the other "big" people in your family can go on a special little trip together.

A grandmother is someone to mother your mother when she needs it.

A grandfather is to fix things your father never finds time to fix, like your tippy tricycle seat and the loose wheel on your racing car.

A grandmother is to say how wonderful, how clever, how bright you are when you show her the pictures you painted at school and read her the book you learned to read and give her the pin dish you made out of clay.

A grandmother is to write you real letters in the mail before anyone else even understands that you can read.

Grandparents are to send you the kind of birthday cards that always have money in them.

Grandparents are to go to visit overnight all by yourself when you need to get away from it all for a while and you're not old enough to go anywhere else.

A grandfather is to tell you about how you could get a double-dip cone for a nickel when he was a little boy and then buy you one with a dip of licorice and a dip of chocolate swirl even though it costs 87 cents.

A grandmother is to sew on buttons and mend your sweaters and wash the baby's diapers if she's your mother's mother; a grandmother is "company coming" if she's your father's mother.

Grandparents are for sending you big surprise packages so the mailman says, "Boy, aren't you a lucky guy" when he brings them

Continued on page 42

Continued from page 41

and even if there's clothes in them there's always something neat, too.

Grandparents are someone who likes your family to come and visit even when you have to take along the baby's bassinet and sixty zillion diapers and all those bottles and even the baby.

A grandmother is to say, "Don't you think he might stay up a little later tonight as long as we're here," and it works.

Grandparents are to make your mother happy when they call up long distance for no reason at all except it's Sunday and talk $5.75 worth.

A grandfather is to tell you what it was like in the olden days when there wasn't any television and there were dinosaurs.

Joan Beck

Blessed Is The Man

Blessed is the man for whom a good woman lives, to whom his work is a pleasure, by whom his friends are encouraged, with whom others are comfortable, in whom a clear conscience abides, and through whom his children see God.

Blessed is the man whose strength is enhanced by his tenderness, whose wisdom is empowered by his faith, and whose courage is made complete by his compassion.

Blessed is the man who looks at life with joyful optimism, who listens to his children with eager attentiveness, who enriches his community with creative enthusiasm, who loves his country with grateful loyalty, and who worships his God with unswerving fidelity.

Blessed is the man who brings honor to the word "father," who is a credit to the word "brotherhood," who is a quiet example of the word "peacemaker," and who is a child's perfect image of the word "manhood."

Blessed is the man who confidently builds bridges of understanding, who generously lightens the loads of his fellow man, and who cheerfully brightens each day with words of hope, inspiration and assurance.

Blessed is the man of whom his children often say, "We're glad he's our father;" of whom his wife often says, "I'm glad he's my husband;" of whom his parents often have said, "We're glad he's our son."

William Arthur Ward

If I Had A Boy

If I had a boy, I would say to him: "Son,
Be fair and be square in the race you must run,
Be brave if you lose and be meek if you win,
Be better and nobler than I've ever been,
Be honest and fearless in all that you do,
And honor the name I have given to you."

If I had a boy, I would want him to know
We reap in this life just about as we sow,
And we get what we earn, be it little or great,
Regardless of luck, and regardless of fate.
I would teach him and show him, the best that
    I could,
That it pays to be honest and upright and good.

I would make him a pal and a partner of mine,
And show him the things in this world that are
    fine,
I would show him the things that are wicked
    and bad,
For I figure this knowledge should come from
    his Dad.
I would walk with him, talk with him, play with
    him too,
And to all of my promises strive to be true.

We would grow up together and I'd be a boy
And share in his trouble and share in his joy,
We would work out problems together and then
We would lay out our plans when we both
    would be men.
And oh, what a wonderful joy it would be,
No pleasure in life could be greater to me.

Author Unknown

Parents' Prayer

And parents paused
Beside his bed,
While from their hearts
This prayer they said:

"Dear God,
We pray again tonight
Help us to lead
Our son aright."

John M. Drescher

The Letter

I found the letter the other day while I was trying once again to clean the attic. It was yellowed with age, creased from many readings, and still bore the unmistakable trace of tears shed in the reading. As I spread the letter out on my lap and started reading, I was transported back thirty years in time.

"Dear Daughter,

As I start this letter to you, I am sure you are sound asleep in your own room at home. You are surrounded with all the things that have been dear to you in childhood—your stuffed animals, posters, high school trophies, and prom programs. But when you read this letter, you will be 500 miles away in your college dormitory room. I hope you will grow to love it as you do the room in which you are now dreaming.

You are starting a whole new life now. If you do not like the image you presented in high school, you can change all that. No one knows you there. You are, in a sense, being re-born. Not everyone gets a chance to start all over. Take advantage of it if you feel the need.

You are going from a small town and a little high school to a cosmopolitan environment where many things will be new and strange. Look at each event; examine each thought. Accept those things which you feel will make you a better person and discard those which you know are only superficial and unimportant.

You will learn a lot in college. You will gain knowledge from books and from your teachers. More than this, you will learn how to live with and get along with people from all sorts of homes.

You will rub shoulders with those of different customs, ideas, religions, races. Be tolerant of their differences and learn from them all you can about the other people who live in the world with you.

As you know, I am not a very demonstrative person and it is hard for me to tell you in words how much I love you. Let me just say that in the eighteen years I have known you, I have never had occasion to be ashamed of you in any way. You have always made your mother and me proud and happy, and we know that you will always continue to do so.

Good Luck in this, your newest venture! Although you are leaving home, you will be in our thoughts and prayers daily.

Love,
Dad"

In the thirty years since this letter was penned, I have written my own letter to three children going to college for the first time. I hope that my notes to them helped them as much as my dad's did me.

Winnifred Piper

A Wedding Prayer

Lord Jesus, who hast won our hearts
   And made our lives Thine own,
In this glad hour we lowly kneel
   In prayer before Thy throne:
Unite us now in love to Thee,
   To live for Thee alone.

          Go with us, Saviour, through the years
             With all their paths untrod;
          Far down the future's hidden way
             Shines Faith's sweet light abroad,
          For come what may, one thing we know—
             The faithfulness of God.

Teach us to love Thee as we ought,
   And love each other more
Because we join in love to Thee
   And prove Thy mercy's store;
So may we serve Thee here on earth,
   And then in Heaven adore!

                           Margaret Clarkson

A Lesson In Caring

There was once a very old man whose eyes had become dim, his ears dull of hearing, his knees trembling. When he sat at the table he could hardly hold the spoon and spilled the broth upon the table-cloth, or let it run out of his mouth.

His son and his son's wife were disgusted at this, so the old grandfather at last had to sit in the corner behind the stove, and they gave him his food in an earthenware bowl, and not even enough of it. And he used to look toward the table with tear-filled eyes.

Once, too, his trembling hands could not hold the bowl, and it fell to the ground and broke. The young wife scolded him; but he said nothing and only sighed. Then they bought him a wooden bowl for a few pennies, out of which he had to eat.

They were once sitting thus when the little grandson four years old began to gather together some bits of wood upon the ground. "What are you doing there?" asked the father. "I am making a little trough," answered the child, "for father and mother to eat out of when I am big."

The man and his wife looked at each other for a while, and presently began to cry. They took the old grandfather to the table, and henceforth always let him eat with them, and said nothing if he did spill a little.

                           Grimm's Fairy Tales

A Boy And A Brook

Travel the country roads on a weekend, when school is not in session, particularly the hill roads beside the brooks, and you will see him. The boy beside the brook, the boy with a bait rod or a fly rod and a special light in his eye. Note that it isn't a willow pole he has, nor a twine string with a bent pin. Chances are you can look all season long and never see that fictional young fisherman. If he ever did exist, which is doubtful, he is gone now. This boy beside the brook isn't being picturesque; he's fishing. He probably has a nylon line, and he knows his leaders, his wet flies and dry ones, and the way to use a worm. He also knows the water, the coves, the eddies, the ripples, and he knows fish.

Country boys have been fishing for a long, long time. It's part of their growing up. Listen to a middle-aged man in waders and within five minutes he will say, "When I was a boy" or "Thirty years ago," and tell you the exciting things that happened right over at that bend or at the mouth of that brook. He has special memories, and now and then he will even share them. Not only of fish and fishing, but of sunlight on water, and shad-blow in bloom, and misty dawns.

If you ever wondered why fishing is probably the most popular sport in this country, watch that boy beside the brook and you will learn. If you are really perceptive you will. For he already knows that fishing is only one part fish. Unless you too were a fisherman when you were young you may never know the other components, but you can sense them a little, just watching. That boy probably won't tell you. He's a little bashful about such things. But he will remember, all his years. And so will you, just seeing him, seeing that look in his eyes.

Hal Borland

To Husband And Wife

Preserve sacredly the privacies of your own house, your married state and your heart. Let no one ever presume to come between you or share the joys or sorrows that belong to you two alone.

With mutual help, build your quiet world, not allowing your dearest earthly friend to be the confidant of aught that concerns your domestic peace. Let moments of alienation, if they occur, be healed at once. Never, never speak of it outside; but to each other confess, and all will come out right. Never let the morrow's sun still find you at variance. Renew and renew your vow. It will do you good; and thereby your minds will grow together contented in that love which is stronger than death, and you will be truly one.

Author Unknown

My Mother's Hands

When I was younger I often wondered why her hands were so large. They were the largest woman's hands I have ever seen—much larger than the ordinary man's hands. They were hands whose nails never knew the glamour of polish or the efficient touch of a manicurist's file. She always clipped the nails with scissors for this was the quickest way, and they were cut very close for she said long nails interfered with her work.

They were not always large hands, however, for when she was a young girl she said she had lovely hands and she wasn't ashamed of them then. How many times have I seen gloves on those hands! They were never seen in public without gloves for she was determined that no stranger was to see her rough, workworn hands.

To me those hands seemed the most beautiful ones in the world, and I wondered how she could have ever been ashamed of them—hands that had reared nine children; hands that could pick two hundred pounds of cotton a day, or hoe an acre of potatoes, as easily and willingly as they could prepare three tempting meals a day; hands whose very touch could ease a sick child's pain; hands always so eager to extend sympathy and help anyone in distress; hands that had the magic touch to lead so many to a richer, more abundant life.

Now I know why her hands were so large—she just couldn't have done so much with smaller hands!

Hugh W. Phillips

Tommy's Essay

A gray sweater hung limply on Tommy's empty desk, a reminder of the dejected boy who had just followed his classmates from our third grade room. Soon Tommy's parents would arrive for a conference on his failing school work and disruptive behavior. Neither parent knew that I had summoned the other.

Tommy, an only child, had always been happy, co-operative, and an excellent student. How could I convince his father and mother that his recent failing grades were a brokenhearted child's reaction to his adored parents' separation and pending divorce?

Tommy's mother entered and took one of the chairs I had placed near my desk. Soon the father arrived. Good! At least they were concerned enough to be prompt. A look of surprise and irritation passed between them, and then they pointedly ignored each other.

As I gave a detailed account of Tommy's behavior and school-work, I prayed for the right words to bring these two together, to help them see what they were doing to their son. But somehow the words didn't come. Perhaps if they saw one of his smudged, care-lessly done papers—

I found a crumpled tearstained sheet stuffed in the back of his desk. It was an English paper. Both sides were covered, not with the assignment, but with a single sentence scribbled over and over.

Silently I smoothed it out and gave it to Tommy's mother. She read it and then handed it to her husband. He frowned. Then his face softened. He studied the scrawled words for what seemed an eternity.

At last he folded the paper carefully, placed it in his pocket, and then reached for his wife's outstretched hand. She wiped the tears from her cheeks and smiled up at him. My own eyes were brimming, but neither seemed to notice. He helped her with her coat and they left together.

In His own way, God had given me the words to reunite that family. He had guided me to a sheet of yellow notebook paper covered with the anguished outpouring of a small boy's heart.

The words? "Dear Mother . . . Dear Daddy . . . I love you . . . I love you . . . I love you. . . ."

Jane Lindstrom

My Father's Watch

There is within my treasure chest
A keepsake that I prize,
It doesn't occupy much space
Because it's small in size.

It is my father's pocket watch
That I got before he died,
He wore the watch for many years
With a special kind of pride.

You see, he got it from his father
So I fondle it with care,
And after all these many years
It really is quite rare.

My father always wore the watch
In a pocket of his vest,
From a buttonhole a golden chain
Hung down upon his chest.

So I look again at this old watch
And in my heart I know,
I'll pass it on someday with tears
When my time comes to go.

Raymond Henry Schreiner

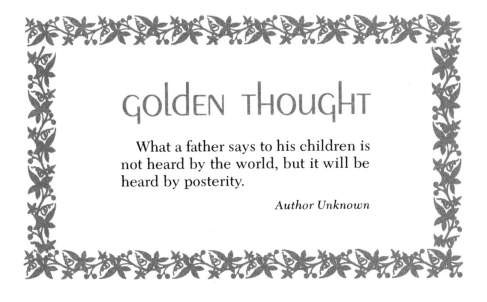

GOLDEN THOUGHT

What a father says to his children is
not heard by the world, but it will be
heard by posterity.

Author Unknown

Let's Read It Together
the children's corner

The Uninvited Dinner Guest

"Is that you, Mom?" eleven-year-old Jennie asked. The rustling in the bushes sounded as though her mother were returning to camp. But there was no answer. Jennie turned to see what had made the noise. Her four-year-old sister Marnie was close by, playing happily with some pinecones she'd found that morning.

A quick look around the campsite indicated nothing out of the ordinary. But suddenly, Jennie noticed out of the corner of her eye something moving where the foliage thinned out. She whirled around. Staring back at her from the edge of the clearing was the biggest black bear she'd ever seen.

Jennie was so frightened she couldn't move. Mom was gathering firewood for their evening meal, and Dad was across the lake fishing. They had left her in camp to take care of Marnie.

Although she was still frightened, Jennie's heart gradually stopped racing. But it was obvious that the bear wasn't frightened at all. In fact, it looked positively delighted at the thought of a good meal. Jennie saw the bear sniffing and then staring at the food pack that Dad had not yet pulled up into the tree. Then the animal ambled in the direction of the food. However, to reach the pack, it had to pass between Marnie and herself.

"Don't move, Marnie," Jennie cautioned. "There's a bear coming but he only wants some food." She tried to keep the fear out of her voice. The last thing she wanted right now was to have her little sister become frightened and start crying. Jennie wouldn't have blamed her though. She wished she felt as brave and as confident as she tried to sound. Keeping her eyes on the bear, Jennie whispered, "Look, Marnie, he must like Mom's cooking. See how he gobbles it all up."

Jennie had read that black bears did not usually attack people, but she didn't really want to put that theory to the test. Maybe the animal would go away on its own. On the other hand, it didn't seem right to sit back and let it eat all their food. As she clenched her fists in frustration, Jennie realized that she was still holding a saucepan lid in her right hand.

Yesterday when they had made their first portage, bypassing Moose Rapids, they had talked with some campers just returning from a trip into the lakes. Jennie had listened keenly when the travelers told of their experiences with the black bears occasionally found in the park. "They're more of a nuisance than a menace," they declared. She remembered laughing out loud when one of the women had told of scaring away a bear by clanging two pots together.

But it didn't seem quite so funny now. *Still, if it worked for that woman,* she reasoned, *why won't it work for me?* The problem was that the pots were on the other side of the campsite. She glanced at her sister. Marnie was sitting still, fascinated by the noises the big black hulk was making as it ate.

Jennie didn't want to turn her back on the bear to get the pot, so she had to walk backward. Carefully putting one foot down, then the other, she started. She was almost there when suddenly she fell down with a thump. She had tripped over a bedroll. Hearing the thud, the bear looked up, put his snout into the air, and sniffed a couple of times. To Jennie's immense relief, that was all. Apparently the lure of the food was just too much. He went back to it with satisfied grunts and juicy slurps.

Jennie proceeded more cautiously this time. When her foot finally nudged something metallic, she knelt down and carefully picked up the closest pot and banged the lid and pot together as hard as she could. Her hands stung from the constant banging, but she didn't stop.

At the first clang, the bear stopped eating and seemed startled at the noise. Then, picking up the last bag of cookies, it sauntered off into the forest. Jennie continued clanging until she was sure it was far away.

Then dropping the mangled pot, she collapsed in a heap beside Marnie who was clapping her hands. *At least someone is amused by the episode,* thought Jennie. She wondered what Mom and Dad would think. She looked at the ruined food sack and hoped that Dad had been successful with his fishing.

At that moment Mom came running into camp, her arms full of firewood. "I just saw the biggest black bear I've ever seen," she gasped, out of breath from running. "I was afraid it would come here and . . ."

Then she stopped as she caught sight of the remains of their food pack and the battered pot. With a feeling of relief and gratitude Mom's imagination completed the rest of the story.

Geraldine Brook

Make Believe Lion

Today I'll be a lion
Outside the kitchen door
And when the neighbor's dog comes near
I'll give a scarey roar.
I'll crawl along the garden grass
Then hide behind a tree
Where I can blink my yellow eyes
To spot an enemy.
I'll use my paws to scratch the ground
And swish my ropey tail
When inching right beneath my nose
Is a funny little snail.
To be a lion is lots of fun
And brings me so much joy,
But when lunch time comes I'm glad that I
Am Mother's little boy.

Dorothy E. Zimmerman

Girlchild

I remember well my tiny babe
born one eve in March, now long ago,
but it seems as only yesterday
the nurses tied into her hair . . . a bow!

Fascinated, I enjoyed my imp
following kitty cats on summer days,
wheat blonde hair and saucy eyes of blue,
yes, I remember her when she was two.

But days of swings and sandbox joys are past
and little girls grow up and leave their toys
as swish hairdos replace the ponytail
and thoughts turn now to "heels"
and dates with boys.

Although tomorrow she will be fifteen
and lovely womanhood around her swirls,
I'll have to pinch myself to see her grown,
for Mamas still remember little girls.

Miriam Woolfolk

Daily Life

Give us day by day our daily bread.
Luke 11:3

My Work

Let me but do my work from day to day,
In fields, or forest, at the desk or loom,
In roaring market place or tranquil room.
Let me find it in my heart to say,
When vagrant wishes beckon me astray,
"This is my work—my blessing, not my doom—
Of all who live I am the one by whom
This work can best be done in my own way."
Then I shall see it, not too great or small
To suit my spirit and arouse my powers.
Then shall I cheerfully greet the laboring hours
And cheerfully turn, when long shadows fall
At eventide, to play and love the rest.
Because I know for me my work is best.

Henry van Dyke

Teach Us To Number Our Days

When Brooks Adams, the son of Charles Francis Adams, was eight he wrote in his diary: "Went fishing with my father; the most glorious day of my life," and through the next forty years he made repeated references to that day and the influence it had on his life.

The father, who was Abraham Lincoln's ambassador to England, recorded about the day: "Went fishing with my son; a day wasted."

Which illustrates the reasonableness of Psalm 90:12, "So teach us to number our days, that we may apply our hearts unto wisdom."

Author Unknown

Back Through The Years

Back through the years I go
To a summertime in yesterday,
Where stacks of hay and sheaves of grain
Thrilled my childhood play.

Where kittens played in the old, red barn—
The smell of fresh-mown hay—
Hidden nests in the loft
Where speckled hens would lay.

Walks in the meadow and orchard
Where little, wild things play,
And gentle sheep are grazing—
Wild birds sing a roundelay.

Back through the years I go
For a time, forgetting today—
Where a little girl and her playmates
Forever and ever will stay.

Lucille Crumley

Our Job

The choices we make each day of the week,
The paths that we take, the goals that we seek,
The kind of persons one day we will be
Is daily determined by you and me.

Each thought that we think, each word that we say
Affect our tomorrows in some strange way.
Each task that we finish, if it's well done,
Prepares us to tackle a bigger one.

For each of us has a talent or two,
A chance to make good on the jobs we do;
A measure of time to squander or use
Is given to us—it's our job to choose.

William Arthur Ward

Attic Dreams

The attic was my kingdom
When I was a little girl.
All it's mysteries lured me
And made my young heart whirl.

I loved it in the attic—
I didn't mind the dust and heat;
For no one there bothered me,
And liberty was sweet.

A world of dreams and history
In trunks whose locks would yield.
I was Queen of this domain
And my scepter I would wield.

Just ten narrow, wooden steps—
The turn of a rusty key—
No chores or grownups here—
My attic dreams soared free.

Lucille Crumley

You Cannot Tell

The morning that you fear to greet
May turn into a day so sweet
That flowers bloom beneath your feet;
You cannot tell.

The cup you so much dread to drink
May prove less bitter than you think
As you pause at water's brink;
You cannot tell.

The rocky road your feet must climb
That seems beyond your strength this time
May lead you to a height sublime
And be well.

Lois Mae Cuhel

Dragon Sea

The sea is a thirsty dragon
lapping the rocks and jetties
with a giant wet tongue,
gobbling up pebbles and shells
as it erases my footsteps on the shore.
Never satisfied, it crashes
and grumbles, roars and mutters,
ever thirsty, ever hungry.
Only the circling gulls alert
for scraps or fish
are unafraid.

Jean Conder Soule

Summer Rain

Thank You, Lord, for quick, cool rain,
For chilly drops that pelt
My sun-warmed face,
For fragrant smell of clean-washed air,
For shivery flecks sharp-felt
On shoulders as I race
To snatch my wash from swaying line.
Dampened? Some. No pain!
The air is cleansed, refreshed, renewed.
Lord, I love your rain!

Annice Harris Brown

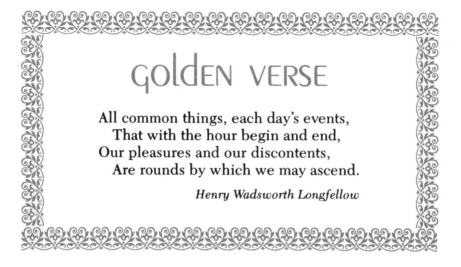

GOLDEN VERSE

All common things, each day's events,
   That with the hour begin and end,
Our pleasures and our discontents,
   Are rounds by which we may ascend.

Henry Wadsworth Longfellow

GOLDEN NUGGET

I should never have made my success in life if I had not bestowed upon the least thing I have ever undertaken, the same attention and care that I have bestowed upon the greatest.

Charles Dickens

Water-Lilies

On that quiet Sabbath morning
　　As we passed the river by,
Saw we choirs of angels sending
　　Perfumed praises to the sky . . .
Snowy-petalled water-lilies
　　Swaying in the breeze,
Solomon in all his glory
　　Not arrayed as one of these:

Wonderous flowers of the water,
　　What a sermon they can preach!
Growing there by man unaided,
　　Words of wisdom they can teach!
Pushing upwards, roots entangled,
　　Mounting higher all the while,
Until they emerge triumphant
　　To receive God's blessed smile.

Dorothy M. Cahoon

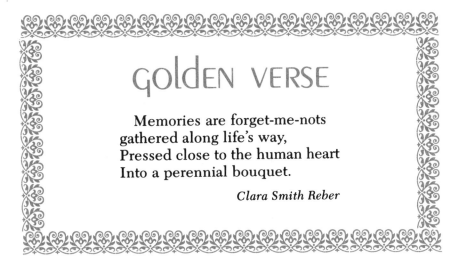

GOLDEN VERSE

Memories are forget-me-nots
gathered along life's way,
Pressed close to the human heart
Into a perennial bouquet.

Clara Smith Reber

GOldEN NUGGETS

A successful man is one who has tried, not cried; who has worked, not dodged; who has shouldered responsibility, not evaded it; who has gotten under the burden instead of standing off, looking on, and giving advice.

Elbert Hubbard

One of the most tragic things I know about human nature is that all of us tend to put off living. We are all dreaming of some magical rose garden over the horizon—instead of enjoying the roses that are blooming outside our windows today . . . Life, we learn too late, is in the living, in the tissue of every day and hour.

Dale Carnegie

Happiness is as a butterfly, which, when pursued, is always just beyond your grasp, but which, if you will sit down quietly, may alight upon you.

Happiness in this world, when it comes, comes incidentally. Make it the object of pursuit, and it leads us a wild-goose chase, and is never attained.

Nathaniel Hawthorne

He who allows a day to pass without practicing generosity or enjoying life's pleasure is like a blacksmith's bellows—he breathes but does not live.

Lowell Thomas

The WickeR Picnic HampeR

As we were leaving church last Sunday, I noticed a dear little elderly lady bent like a weathered tree caning her way carefully down the steps to a waiting taxi. No one came to her aid. No one offered to take her home, and as my family and I got settled comfortably in our new luxury car and headed toward one of the town's finest restaurants, my thoughts went whirling backward to Grandma and Grandpa.

They never failed to attend church. Throughout the warm months, Grandma would arise at 5:30 on Sundays and prepare fried chicken, potato salad, scrub and polish a dozen or more crisp apples, slice cheese and wrap it in waxed paper, and tuck it all into a huge wicker picnic hamper. Last of all would come a stack of blue and white checkered linen napkins and a matching cloth, and two fresh fruit pies baked the night before. Then Grandpa took his mandolin from the mantel and whisked it and the wicker hamper into the trunk of the old Essex, and off to church we'd go.

After the services, Grandpa would make the rounds of the congregation gathering up every waif, widow, widower, spinster, or just plain old lonely person that he could find.

"Come to the park for a picnic," he'd say jovially. "Pearl fixed a ton more than our little family will be able to eat up in a month of Sundays!"

Grandpa would get everyone settled comfortably at the tables or on blankets on the lawn, and Mother, Grandma, and sometimes Papa would unpack the food treasure. After dinner, Grandpa would round up all the "younguns" he could find and set up the croquet set. When the last wicket was conquered, he'd take his mandolin and we'd all sing together, or often he would encourage the guests to tell us tales out of their memories of the long, long ago.

What happy Sundays those were—sharing with the lonely and family-less, and showing in some small way that we cared about them as folks with strengths and weaknesses, joys and emptinesses, human beings like ourselves.

My thoughts were jolted back by the lurching halt of the car and as I walked up the stone steps of the restaurant, I silently vowed: "Next Sunday the little lady with the cane will have a place to eat a nice dinner, company with someone who cares and wants to know her, and a ride home in a nice new car."

Phyllis Walk

If —

If you can keep your head when all about you
    Are losing theirs and blaming it on you;
If you can trust yourself when all men doubt you,
    But make allowance for their doubting too;
If you can wait and not be tired by waiting,
    Or, being lied about, don't deal in lies,
Or, being hated, don't give way to hating,
    And yet don't look too good, nor talk too wise;

If you can dream, and not make dreams your master;
    If you can think, and not make thoughts your aim;
If you can meet with Triumph and Disaster
    And treat those two imposters just the same;
If you can bear to hear the truth you've spoken
    Twisted by knaves to make a trap for fools,
Or watch the things you gave your life to, broken,
    And stoop, and build them up with wornout tools;

If you can make one heap of all your winnings
    And risk it on one turn of pitch-and-toss,
And lose, and start again at your beginnings
    And never breathe a word about your loss;
If you can force your heart and nerve and sinew
    To serve your turn long after they are gone,
And so hold on when there is nothing in you
    Except the Will which says to them: "Hold on!"

If you can talk with crowds and keep your virtue,
    Or walk with kings—nor lose the common touch—
If neither foes nor loving friends can hurt you,
    If all men count with you, but none too much;
If you can fill the unforgiving minute
    With sixty seconds' worth of distance run,
Yours is the Earth and everything that's in it,
    And—which is more—you'll be a Man, my son!

Rudyard Kipling

A Thing Of Beauty Is A Joy Forever

A thing of beauty is a joy forever:
Its loveliness increases; it will never
Pass into nothingness; but still
　　will keep
A bower quiet for us, and a sleep
Full of sweet dreams, and health,
　　and quiet breathing.
　　　　. . . yes, in spite of all,
Some shape of beauty moves away
　　the pall
From our dark spirits. Such the sun,
　　the moon,
Trees old, and young, sprouting a
　　shady boon
For simple sheep; and such are
　　daffodils
With the green world they live in;
　　and clear rills
That for themselves a cooling
　　covert make
'Gainst the hot season; the mid
　　forest brake,
Rich with a sprinkling of fair
　　musk-rose blooms:
And such too is the grandeur
　　of the dooms
We have imagined for the mighty
　　dead;
All lovely tales that we have
　　heard or read:
An endless fountain of immortal
　　drink,
Pouring unto us from the
　　heaven's brink.

John Keats

The Tree

I stand here lonely—
Chained to this spot.
I am old and tired.

I have watched generations
   pass through this valley.
I have seen life begin . . .
And I have seen it end.

I have watched families
   come and go.
I have held children high
   in my boughs.
And I have seen them fall
   —and cry.

I have lent my shade to couples
So deeply in love,
They shared themselves with me.

I have felt the gentle showers
   of spring
And the harsh storms of winter.
And I have long outlived man.

For a man pulls up roots
   and changes homes.
He is not content where he is.
I was planted here.
And my roots have found
   their place.

Vicki Lynne Sauers

The Rose Beyond The Wall

Near a shady wall a rose once grew
    Budded and blossomed in God's free light,
Watered and fed by morning dew
    Shedding its sweetness day and night.

As it grew and blossomed fair and tall,
    Slowly rising to loftier height,
It came to a crevice in the wall
    Through there shown a beam of light.

Onward it crept with added strength
    With never a thought of fear or pride
It followed the light through the crevice's length
    And unfolded itself on the other side.

Shall claim of death cause us to grieve
    And make our courage faint and fall?
Nay! Let us faith and hope receive,
    The rose still grows beyond the wall.

Paulyne M. Penrod

Summer Blue

How very strange that summer's eyes
Should match the blueness of the skies,
Perhaps that's why she seems to care
For bluebells plaited through her hair.
Folks take it as a welcome sign
To see the morning-glory vine
Twine in and out her window-sill,
As sunlight peeps across the hill.
No day goes by she doesn't take
A stroll about the sapphire lake,
With not the slightest smudge or wrinkle,
To spoil her gown of periwinkle.
And that is why I know it's true,
That summer's favorite shade is BLUE!

Grace E. Easley

GOLDEN THOUGHTS

Great occasions for serving God come seldom, but little ones surround us daily.

Francis De Sales

An open mind affords the opportunity of dropping a worthwhile thought into it.

Author Unknown

Iron rusts from disuse, stagnant water loses its purity and in cold weather becomes frozen; even so does inaction sap the vigors of the mind.

Leonardo da Vinci

Life is a mirror: if you frown at it, it frowns back; if you smile, it returns the greeting.

Thackeray

Nothing great was ever achieved without enthusiasm.

Ralph Waldo Emerson

Our Life

God gives us days, one by one,
    each day significant
    a part of His plan for
    our contribution to our world
    our offering to Him.

God gives life, day by day,
    made of small opportunities
    (now and then, greater ones)
    choices to make
    difficulties to overcome.

He makes available to us
    His grace, His power
    guidance for each choice
    strength for our daily walk
    day added to day—our life.

Leota Campbell

Time And Money

As for a little more money and a little more time, why it's ten to one, if either one or the other would make you one whit happier. If you had more time, it would be sure to hang heavily. It is the working man who is the happy man. Man was made to be active, and he is never so happy as when he is so. It is the idle man who is the miserable man. What comes of holidays, and far too often of sight-seeing, but evil? Half the harm that happens is on those days. And, as for money—Don't you remember the old saying, "Enough is as good as a feast?" Money never made a man happy yet, nor will it. There is nothing in its nature to produce happiness. The more a man has, the more he wants. Instead of its filling a vacuum, it makes one. If it satisfies one want, it doubles and trebles that want another way. That was a true proverb of the wise man, rely upon it: "Better is little with the fear of the Lord, than great treasure, and trouble therewith."

Benjamin Franklin

LET'S READ IT TOGETHER
the children's corner

Hortense And The Gasoline Machine

Hortense was a gray mare who worked for Farmer Brown. She had lived on the farm all of her life. Hortense was happy on the farm. She liked working for Farmer Brown. She liked pulling the plow, mowing the grass and hauling hay in the big wagon.

However, one day Farmer Brown said:

"Hortense old girl, you've served your time. You must take it easy; you're long past your prime."

Farmer Brown took the halter off Hortense's neck and turned her into the back pasture.

When Hortense had nothing else to do, she listened to the shiny, red tractor, chugging, chugging, chugging around over the farm, pulling the plow, mowing the grass, hauling things for Farmer Brown. Doing all the chores Hortense used to do. Hortense grew jealous of the tractor. She wanted to go over and kick its tires. She hoped it would break down. Then Farmer Brown would have to take Hortense back and let her do all the things she loved to do.

"I'm getting useless, as useless can be," Hortense said to herself one morning. It seems anyone should be able to see, that even a horse goes into a tizzy if she isn't working, if she isn't kept busy.

Then, one day the big gasoline truck came to fill up the pump at Farmer Brown's barnlot. Hortense, who had nothing better to do, went over to the fence to watch. She saw the truck driver talking to Farmer Brown. Then, the driver shook his head, got into the truck and drove away without even taking the big hose off the truck.

Hortense wondered what was going on. Why didn't Farmer Brown buy gasoline as he usually did? Hortense thought about this until Farmer Brown came to lead her back to the barn.

"Well, old girl," said Farmer Brown, as he put her in her stall. "It's sad but it's true, there's an energy shortage the whole country through. I put you to pasture to live out your days, but now I have to return to old ways. Tractors need fuel, now in short supply; horses eat hay, of which I have plenty. So back to the plow and the mowing machine, you burn only hay not scarce gasoline."

So Hortense went back to plowing the furrows so straight and mowing the grass right up to the gate. Hortense was so proud to be useful once more. She danced and she pranced through each single chore.

"Hortense, old girl, you're simply great," Farmer Brown said as he hitched her up one morning. "There's no denying the fact that you rate as the best friend a farmer ever had. I see now that for you this work's not so bad. I hope you understand the change in our pace. Sometimes it's the steady and slow ones who win the race."

Hortense tossed her mane and began to pull the plow down the furrow. Indeed work was not bad. It was standing alone in the pasture that had made her so sad.

Shannon Graham

Hush!

Hush! Stop the big sounds,
Listen to the small.
Can you hear the leaves brush
Against the garden wall?

Can you hear the busy hum
Of a bumblebee?
Can you hear the grasses
Swishing lazily?

Can you hear the tapping
Of a woodpecker's bill?
Can you hear the splashing
As the brook runs down the hill?

Can you hear the little sounds
About us everywhere?
Oh, there's special joy in them
For all who listen well and care.

Solveig Paulson Russell

Fireflies

Fireflies flitting 'round about
   with tiny lanterns glowing,
Guardians of the summer night
   So silently coming, going.

Fireflies flitting here and there
In trees, and shrubs and grass,
Are playing tag with children
As they have for ages past.

Rhena S. LaFever

Boy On A Country Road

Look at the patches on both his knees
   And the toes kicked out of his shoes.
And old blue sweater flung over his shoulder
   While the seat of his pants hangs loose.

His collar is never buttoned at all—
   His pockets are empty of money,
But he knows every bird call in the spring
   And where wild bees store their honey.

The ragged old hat is never on straight—
   He whistles and doesn't care.
And if his face is smudged with dirt
   It matches the un-combed hair.

His lips are pursed for a lilting tune
   To the dog running by his side,
And nothing could ever make him more happy
   Than tramping the countryside.

Velta Myrle Allen

American Heritage

Happy is that people, whose God is the LORD.
Psalms 144:15

One United People

Independent America is not composed of detached and distant territories, but is one connected, fertile, widespreading country. Providence has blessed it with a variety of soils and produce, and has watered it with innumerable streams. A succession of navigable waters forms a chain around our borders, binding us together . . . while the most noble rivers in the world, running at convenient distances, present our people with highways for easy communication and exchange of commodities.

And . . . Providence has been pleased to give this one connected country to one united people . . . speaking the same language . . . attached to the same principles of government . . . similar in their manners and customs . . . a united people who, by their joint counsels, arms and efforts, fighting side by side throughout a long and bloody war, have nobly established their liberty and independence.

This country and this people seem to have been made for each other, and it appears to be the design of Providence that a heritage so proper and convenient should never be split into a number of unsocial, jealous and alien sovereignties.

For all general purposes, we are uniformly one people, each individual citizen everywhere enjoying the same national rights, privileges and protection.

John Jay, America's First Chief Justice

Old Covered Bridge

There's an old covered bridge in my memory
Spanning a river wide,
And I think of the folks who have traveled through
Safe to the other side;
Where horses rested and the swallows nested,
And shy fish swam below—
Yes, a page from the past is the covered bridge,
From the book of long ago.

Doris Philbrick

A Long Life—A Good Life

You ask if I would agree to live my seventy or rather seventy-three years over again? To which I say yea. I think with you that it is a good world on the whole; that it has been framed on a principle of benevolence, and more pleasure than pain dealt out to us. There are, indeed, (who might say nay) gloomy and hypochondriac minds, inhabitants of diseased bodies, disgusted with the present, and despairing of the future; always counting that the worst will happen, because it may happen. To these I say, how much pain have cost us the evils which have never happened! My temperament is sanguine. I steer my bark with Hope in the head, leaving Fear astern. My hopes, indeed, sometimes fail; but not oftener than the forebodings of the gloomy. There are, I acknowledge, even in the happiest life, some terrible convulsions, heavy set-offs against the opposite page of the account. I have often wondered for what good end the sensations of grief could be intended. All our other passions, within proper bounds, have a useful object. And the perfection of the moral character is, not in a stoical apathy, so hypocritically vaunted, and so untruly too, because impossible, but in a just equilibrium of all the passions. I wish the pathologists then, would tell us what is the use of grief in the economy, and of what good it is the cause, proximate or remote.

Thomas Jefferson

The Inscription At Mount Vernon

Washington, the brave, the wise, the good,
Supreme in war, in council, and in peace,
Valiant without ambition, discreet without fear,
Confident without presumption.
In disaster, calm; in success, moderate;
In all, himself.
    The hero, the patriot, the Christian.
    The father of nations, the friend of mankind,
    Who, when he had won all, renounced all,
    And sought in the bosom of his family
    And of nature, retirement,
    And in the hope of religion, immortality.

First In War, First In Peace

First in war, first in peace, and first in the
hearts of his countrymen, he was second to none
in the humble and endearing scenes of private
life. Pious, just, humane, temperate and sincere;
uniform, dignified and commanding, his example was as edifying to all around him, as were
the effects of that example lasting.

Henry Lee

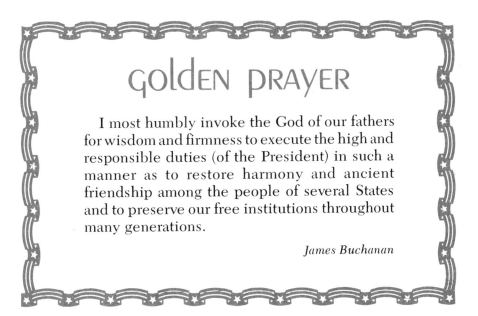

GOLDEN PRAYER

I most humbly invoke the God of our fathers
for wisdom and firmness to execute the high and
responsible duties (of the President) in such a
manner as to restore harmony and ancient
friendship among the people of several States
and to preserve our free institutions throughout
many generations.

James Buchanan

Our Most Famous Postmasters

Benjamin Franklin and Abraham Lincoln—two of America's most famous men—were postmasters.

Although they were born 103 years apart, they had a lot in common. Both came from humble homes, both taught themselves, both became important leaders, and both fought for freedom.

Born in Boston in 1706, Benjamin Franklin went to school for only two years. He became a candlemaker at the age of 10. He did not like this work so he learned to be a printer in his brother's shop.

Young Ben read many books he borrowed from friends. In later years, he looked back on his desire to learn, and started America's first public library, in Philadelphia.

He left home at 17 and went to Philadelphia, where he found work in another print shop. In a few years he owned his own newspaper. He was named postmaster of Philadelphia when he was 31.

Mail was sent in colonial days by post riders on horseback, by boat, and by stagecoach. Franklin tried to speed up the mails because he knew good mail service would help the country grow strong.

Franklin helped run the Royal posts (mail routes) from 1753 until he was removed from his job in 1774. The colonies began their own postal service and appointed Franklin as their Postmaster General. Then his chief duties were to improve the mails to help General Washington's troops keep in touch with each other. He stayed in that job until he was sent to France as a special representative for the new United States of America.

Great men often learn by reading about other famous leaders. Years later, young Abe Lincoln read Franklin's story of his life.

Lincoln was born in 1809, and his early life was spent at the edge of the western frontier.

Lincoln, like Franklin, taught himself by borrowing books from friends whenever he could.

When Lincoln was 24, he was named postmaster of New Salem, Illinois, in 1833. Mail service in Illinois in those days was little better than the colonial service under Franklin. Mail was carried chiefly by coaches and boats. Postmaster Lincoln's mail came just once a week, and when people did not pick it up at his post office, he would take it to them. He usually carried the mail in his hat.

In Lincoln's day, before stamps were printed, a postmaster wrote the cost of sending a letter in the upper corner where we now put our stamp. The person who received the letter had to pay for it, not the person who sent it.

Each page cost 6¢ to send the first 30 miles. To send a letter 80 miles, it cost 10¢, and a page going 400 miles cost 18¾¢.

Postmaster Lincoln kept his postage money in an old blue sock, and his safe was a wooden chest under the counter in his office.

He got very little pay for his work because very little mail went through his office. However, he read all the newspapers and got to know many people in his part of the state. This helped him get elected state representative, then Congressman. He was elected President in 1860.

Only one other American appears on more U.S. stamps than Franklin and Lincoln. That man is George Washington.

Author Unknown

Can Prayer Save America?

In the days of the Civil War, a personal friend of Abraham Lincoln was a visitor at the White House. "I had been spending three weeks with Mr. Lincoln as his guest. One night—it was just after the Battle of Bull Run—I was restless and could not sleep . . . from the private room where the president slept, I heard low tones, for the door was partly open. Instinctively I wandered in, and there I saw a sight which I have never forgotten. It was the president, kneeling before an open Bible . . . his back was toward me. I shall never forget his prayer: 'Oh, thou God, that heard Solomon in the night when he prayed and cried for wisdom, hear me. I cannot lead these people, I cannot guide the affairs of this nation without Thy help. . . . O God, hear me and save this nation.'"

George Washington, our first president, who prayed in the snow at Valley Forge said, "The event is in the hands of God." When the tide of battle was unfavorable, Washington said, "How will it end? God will direct."

When the leaders of our country assembled to write the constitution, it was proposed by Benjamin Franklin that each session be opened with prayer. Franklin said, "I have lived a long time, and the longer I live the more convincing proof I see of this truth—that God governs the affairs of men. And if a sparrow cannot fall to the ground without His notice, is it possible that an empire can rise without His aid?"

Our nation today is great because it was founded by men who feared God and men who believed in prayer.

Author Unknown

Lincoln

A man of great ability, pure patriotism, un-
selfish nature, full of forgiveness to his enemies,
bearing malice toward none, he proved to be the
man above all others for the struggle through
which the nation had to pass to place itself
among the greatest in the family of nations. His
fame will grow brighter as time passes and his
great, great work is better understood.

Ulysses S. Grant

Lincoln, The Man Of The People

The color of the ground was in him, the red earth,
The smack and tang of elemental things:
The rectitude and patience of the cliff,
The good-will of the rain that loves all leaves,
The friendly welcome of the wayside well,
The courage of the bird that dares the sea,
The gladness of the wind that shakes the corn,
The pity of the snow that hides all scars,
The secrecy of streams that make their way
Under the mountain to the rifted rock,
The tolerance and equity of light
That gives as freely to the shrinking flower
As to the great oak flaring to the wind—
To the grave's low hill as to the Matterhorn
That shoulders out the sky.

So came the Captain with the mighty heart;
And when the judgment thunders split the house,
Wrenching the rafters from their ancient rest,
He held the ridgepole up, and spiked again
The rafters of the Home. He held his place—
Held the long purpose like a growing tree—
Held on through blame and faltered not at praise—
Towering in calm rough-hewn sublimity.
And when he fell in whirlwind, he went down
As when a lordly cedar, green with boughs,
Goes down with a great shout upon the hills,
And leaves a lonesome place against the sky.

Edwin Markham

gOldEN NOTE

Best Gifts

Julia Ward Howe was so deep in thought that her husband kissed her cheek to rouse her. She smiled gratefully, happy that God had blessed her with many "best gifts" (1 Corinthians 12:31). He had given her a good husband, a fine doctor who healed the sick and helped the blind. And He had blessed her, indeed, with five wonderful children. She had a good, rich, and happy life. If—if only she could share her best gifts with the wounded boys she had seen in the army tents that day.

"I know—" said her husband softly, aware of what set in his wife's pretty head. "War is evil—"

His words pierced her heart and rushed hot tears to her eyes. "So many men were brought in today—" she murmured sadly. "And they are so young—and those walking—what courage! Did you hear them singing?"

Her husband nodded. "John Fremont Clarke was with you today, wasn't he?"

"Yes. He walked alongside me, and even he, strong, brave man that he is, went gushy. 'Listen to them,' he said, 'they're singing an old folk song—'"

"'John Brown's body,'" cut in her husband.

"Yes, but John said something that I simply can't forget—"

"Oh?"

"He said it was a stirring tune, and that if the words were different, it would be a beautiful song." Her lips curled whimsically. "John Fremont Clarke has great ideas. He actually said that I ought to write new words."

"And why not?" asked her husband quickly.

Julia Ward Howe made no promise. But was it really necessary? Pride and love for her beloved country rushed through her heart like a forest fire, placing dreams in her eyes and words in her head. Even if she wanted to, she could not have turned off the stream of words that rushed to her brain.

She was compelled to sit down with pen and paper and pour out, "Mine eyes have seen the glory of the coming of the Lord . . . " And she knew God was with her, placing those words in her head and guiding her hand. And as she wrote the rest of her great poem, "The Battle Hymn of the Republic," she was gratefully certain God was permitting her to share her "best gifts."

Clare Miseles

This Land And Flag

What is the love of country for which our flag stands? Maybe it begins with love of the land itself. It is the fog rolling in with the tide at Eastport, or through the Golden Gate and among the towers of San Francisco. It is the sun coming up behind the White Mountains, over the Green, throwing a shining glory on Lake Champlain and above the Adirondacks. It is the storied Mississippi rolling swift and muddy past St. Louis, rolling past Cairo, pouring down past the levees of New Orleans. It is lazy noontide in the pines of Carolina; it is a sea of wheat rippling in western Kansas; it is the San Francisco peaks far north across the glowing nakedness of Arizona; it is the Grand Canyon, and a little stream coming down out of a New England ridge, in which are trout.

It is men at work. It is the storm-tossed fishermen coming into Gloucester and Provincetown and Astoria. It is the farmer riding his great machine in the dust of harvest, the dairyman going to the barn before sunrise; the lineman mending the broken wire; the miner drilling for the blast. It is the servants of fire in the murky splendor of Pittsburgh, between the Allegheny and the Monongahela; the trucks rumbling through the night, the locomotive engineer bringing the train in on time; the pilot in the clouds, the riveter running along the beam a hundred feet in air. It is the clerk in the office, the housewife doing the dishes and sending the chil-

dren off to school. It is the teacher, doctor, and parson tending and helping, body and soul, for small reward.

It is stories told. It is the Pilgrims dying in their first dreadful winter. It is the minuteman standing his ground at Concord Bridge, and dying there. It is the army in rags, sick, freezing, starving at Valley Forge. It is the wagons and the men on foot going westward over Cumberland Gap, floating down the great rivers, rolling over the great plains. It is the settler hacking fiercely at the primeval forest on his new, his own lands. It is Thoreau at Walden Pond, Lincoln at Cooper Union, and Lee riding home from Appomattox. It is corruption and disgrace, answered always by men who would not let the flag lie in the dust, who have stood up in every generation to fight for the old ideals and the old rights, at risk of ruin or of life itself.

It is the great multitude of people on pilgrimage, common and ordinary people, charged with the usual human failings, yet filled with such a hope as never caught the imaginations and the hearts of any nation on earth before. The hope of liberty. The hope of justice. The hope of a land in which a man can stand straight, without fear, without rancor.

The land and the people and the flag . . . the land a continent, the people of every race, the flag a symbol of what humanity may aspire to when the wars are over and the barriers are down; to these each generation must be dedicated and consecrated anew, to defend with life itself, if need be, but above all, in friendliness, in hope, in courage, to live for.

Author Unknown

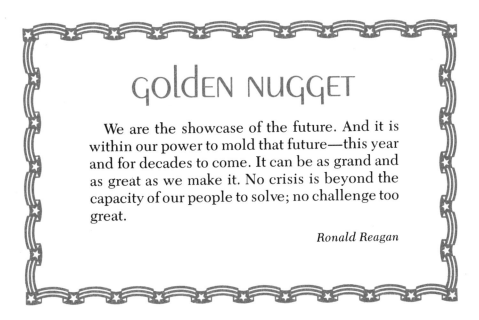

GOLDEN NUGGET

We are the showcase of the future. And it is within our power to mold that future—this year and for decades to come. It can be as grand and as great as we make it. No crisis is beyond the capacity of our people to solve; no challenge too great.

Ronald Reagan

Barbara Frietchie

Up from the meadows rich with corn,
Clear in the cool September morn,

The clustered spires of Frederick stand
Green-walled by the hills of Maryland.

Round about them orchards sweep,
Apple and peach-tree fruited deep,

Fair as a garden of the Lord
To the eyes of the famished rebel horde,

On that pleasant morn of the early fall
When Lee marched over the mountain wall;

Over the mountains winding down,
Horse and foot, into Frederick town.

Forty flags with their silver stars,
Forty flags with their crimson bars,

Flapped in the morning wind: the sun
Of noon looked down, and saw not one.

Up rose old Barbara Frietchie then,
Bowed with her fourscore years and ten;

Bravest of all in Frederick town,
She took up the flag the men hauled down;

In her attic window the staff she set,
To show that one heart was loyal yet.

Up the street came the rebel tread,
Stonewall Jackson riding ahead.

Under his slouched hat left and right
He glanced; the old flag met his sight.

"Halt!"—the dust-brown ranks stood fast.
"Fire!"—out blazed the rifle blast.

It shivered the window, pane and sash;
It rent the banner with seam and gash.

Quick, as it fell, from the broken staff
Dame Barbara snatched the silken scarf.

She leaned far out on the window-sill,
And shook it forth with a royal will.

"Shoot, if you must, this old grey head,
But spare your country's flag," she said.

A shade of sadness, a blush of shame,
Over the face of the leader came;

The nobler nature within him stirred
To life at that woman's deed and word;

"Who touches a hair of yon grey head
Dies like a dog! March on!" he said.

All day long through Frederick street
Sounded the tread of marching feet:

All day long that free flag tost
Over the heads of the rebel host.

Ever its torn folds rose and fell
On the loyal winds that loved it well;

And through the hill-gaps sunset light
Shone over it with a warm good-night.

Barbara Frietchie's work is o'er,
And the rebel rides on his raids no more.

Honor to her! and let a tear
Fall, for her sake, on Stonewall's bier.
Over Barbara Frietchie's grave,
Flag of freedom and union, wave!
Peace, and order, and beauty draw
Round thy symbol of light and law;
And ever the stars above look down
On thy stars below in Frederick town!

John Greenleaf Whittier

A Love Letter From Valley Forge

Much has been written of the dreadful months during late 1777 and early 1778 when the ragged troops of General Washington endured hunger, cold and discouragement at Valley Forge.

But the hardships of the army were made up of more than the problems of a military force facing possible extinction. They were made up of individual tragedies.

These tales do not make history books. But they do deserve attention, for the sacrifice of one man is the whole sacrifice of war itself.

The tale of a Continental soldier named Arthur Carrington encamped those months at Valley Forge is one such tragedy.

Carrington and several other soldiers were sent out from camp to forage for provisions. They made their way to French Creek. Just as they reached the stream—now swollen with the spring rains—a messenger from the Forge encampment caught up with them with a breathless message: "The Redcoats are comin'!"

Carrington spun on his heel. "Follow me! I know where there's a cave in that bluff ahead!" The young soldier led the way quickly.

He could see the cave ahead of them. He had discovered it some time ago on a foraging trip. It was marked by a rock just over the entrance, so well balanced that a man could move it with one hand.

Arthur Carrington threw himself inside the welcome opening just as three shots echoed through the valley. The British had spotted them! He turned to help the others get in. At that moment the rock over the entrance crashed down covering the entrance. He was alone, shut inside. He listened. There wasn't a sound.

He decided to shout. Whether it was his own men outside or the enemy, he realized with an increasing feeling of horror that he needed help.

He shouted. He struck the stone barrier with his fists, stabbed at it with his pocket knife, then his booted feet.

He sat down feeling weak and sapped of strength and courage.

Perhaps his companions had escaped and were back at the Forge right now enlisting help to get him out. Maybe even the British had seen him run into the cave and would be back with help to move the stone. That was surely it. Someone would be back for him.

The hours trailed painfully into days. Arthur Carrington knew at last that no one was coming for him.

He lay back with fever-glazed eyes and parched throat. The only source of air and light to comfort him was a small aperture in the roof of the cave. He stared at it as though it would be the source of some divine aid.

Finally he saw nothing but the image of his young love. Virginia.

He turned on one side. Dear Lord. What would become of her? They were to be married when he returned from the war.

Arthur Carrington pulled himself into a sitting position. He tugged at a scrap of paper that was in his pocket.

He would write a letter to Virginia. Perhaps some day he would be found. He wanted her to know what had happened to him.

Arthur started writing. He didn't stop until the sunlight filtering through the roof's small opening faded into shadow.

He re-read his words. The expedition, the shots, the falling of the rock. All was there. The words went on, "He who has created us must know what is good for us, and we can only submit . . . To know that your heart is mine atones . . . for all I have suffered or can yet suffer . . . I cannot say farewell—there is no farewell to love like ours. This agony will soon be over and I will be free . . . ."

Carrington looked about him. An empty bottle lay against the far wall of the cave. He crawled towards it, rubbed away from the surface the damp sand and pushed the rolled-up letter inside.

The letter stayed where the young Continental soldier had placed it for far longer than he probably could have imagined. His sweetheart never saw it. She died two years after the tragic incident.

It was not until the summer of 1889 that the story of Arthur Carrington came to light. A new granite quarry was being dug in a wild section of country at the Falls of French Creek, when a cave was unearthed. It contained a skeleton. Alongside the gaunt find was a hand-blown green bottle of the Revolutionary era. A letter was crammed inside.

The superintendent of the project, W. W. Potts, ordered the remains carefully removed and took the bottle and letter home for study. The discolored manuscript was addressed to Miss Virginia Randolph of Richmond, Virginia. It was signed by Arthur Carrington of the same city. The date was May 20, 1778.

Potts immediately wrote to a friend in Richmond who sent two old letters written in 1779 by a Rachel Randolph to a girl friend, mentioning the disappearance of the young man and the approaching demise of the young girl.

The friend also replied that the old family burying ground near her house had a monument with the inscription: "Died of a broken heart on the 1st of March 1780. Virginia Randolph, aged 21 years and 9 days. 'Faithful unto death'."

Adi-Kent Thomas Jeffry

Torch Of Liberty

Proud Torch of Liberty lift high
    your flame on every strand,
Illume the way from earth to sky
    in every groping land
Throughout the world, from east to west,
    across the seven seas,
Where trade winds kiss the billow crest,
    where icy north winds freeze.
Your blessed light can not grow dim,
    though foe its strength decry,
For those who seek to follow HIM
    will never let it die.

Ethel P. Travis

Golden Thought

Be sure you put your feet in the right place, then stand firm.

Abraham Lincoln

The Lone Eagle

Great as our space achievements have been—and those who have made them possible—we should never forget the man who probably is our greatest homegrown American hero of the century—Charles A. Lindbergh, the "Lone Eagle," who pioneered our freedom of movement through flight in the first solo nonstop crossing of the Atlantic in 1927. His daring feat in his frail single-engine Spirit of St. Louis forged a flight path that we now take for granted.

On his historic flight, Lindbergh gained some spiritual insights that he later shared with the world in his book, *The Spirit of St. Louis.*

"It is hard to be an agnostic up here in the Spirit of St. Louis," he wrote, "aware of the frailty of man's devices, a part of the universe between its earth and stars. If one dies, all this goes on existing in a plan so perfectly balanced, so wonderfully simple, so incredibly complex that it's far beyond our comprehension—worlds and moons revolving; planets orbiting on suns; suns flung with apparent recklessness through space. There's the infinite magnitude of the universe; there's the infinite detail of its matter—the outer star, the inner atom. And man conscious of it all—a worldly audience to what if not God?"

Author Unknown

Let's Read It Together
the children's corner

America's Folk Heros

There are many heroes and heroines in American folklore. Some of them are real but some of them are only make believe. Here are the most famous ones and the deeds they are noted for.

Rip Van Winkle lived in a small village on the Hudson River. He didn't like to work so his wife nagged him all the time. He went hunting in the mountains to get away from her nagging. There he saw some little men playing nine pins. He sat down to watch them and fell asleep. When he awoke, he returned to the village. The village was much bigger than he had remembered it. The people were wearing strange looking clothes, and he didn't recognize any of them. Everyone was staring at him. They thought his clothes were strange looking, too. He heard a familiar voice and saw a woman who looked like his wife. It was his daughter. Rip had been sleeping for *twenty years!* This story was written by Washington Irving.

Molly Pitcher (1754-1832) Molly Hays was married to a soldier. She went with him into battle and helped nurse the wounded soldiers. At the battle of Monmouth it was very hot. She carried pitcher after pitcher of cold water to the soldiers who were firing the canon. She carried so many pitchers they called her Molly Pitcher. When her husband fell wounded, she took his place and loaded and swabbed his gun. After the battle, General Washington made her "Sergeant Molly Pitcher."

Johnny Appleseed (1774-1845) John Chapman walked barefoot through the Ohio Valley, wearing a tinpot hat and coffee-sack shirt, planting and distributing apple seeds and seedlings in exchange for food and clothing. He bought and distributed religious tracts with any money he was given. His blossoming orchards dotted the land he loved.

Continued on page 88

Continued from page 87

Davy Crockett (1786-1836) was a hunter and trapper who could "whip his weight in wildcats and shoot six cord of bear in one day." He was known for his sense of humor, his tall tales and his political barbs. He fought in the War of 1812 and was a scout for Andrew Jackson. He was elected to Congress three times. He died at the Alamo in Texas.

Lt. Col. George Armstrong Custer (1839-1876) helped to win many battles during the Civil War, but was most famous for his defeat at Little Bighorn. He and 225 men of the 7th Cavalry were killed there. The only survivor was his horse, Comanche. There is a ballad written about Comanche.

Buffalo Bill (1846-1917) William Cody was an Army scout, an Indian fighter, and a Pony Express rider. He killed buffalo to provide meat for the men building the railroad across the country. He became known as Buffalo Bill when he won a buffalo-killing contest. He starred in his own Wild West Show.

Annie Oakley (1860-1926) "Little Sure Shot" could hit dimes in midair and slice playing cards edgewise at 30 paces with her rifle. She became a famous international star touring with Buffalo Bill's Wild West Show.

Paul Bunyan. When woodsmen sat around their campfires at night they told tall tales about Paul Bunyan, a legendary giant. They said he was born in Maine and when he rolled in his sleep he knocked down four square miles of trees. So they built a floating cradle for him and anchored it off Eastport. When he rocked, it caused a tidal wave that wiped out three villages. He moved to Minnesota and Wisconsin because there was more room. There he acquired a blue ox called "Babe." Babe was seven ax handles wide between the eyes and strong enough to haul a forest of logs in one load.

John Henry worked on the Chesapeake & Ohio Railroad in the early 1870's digging tunnels through the mountains. He had a contest with a newly invented steam drill. John Henry drilled two holes with sledge hammers faster than the steam drill could drill one. But John burst a blood vessel and died. The railroad had a hard time getting men to dig their tunnels because the men said they could hear the ghost of John Henry still hammering.

Can you think of any other folk heroes? Who is *your* favorite?

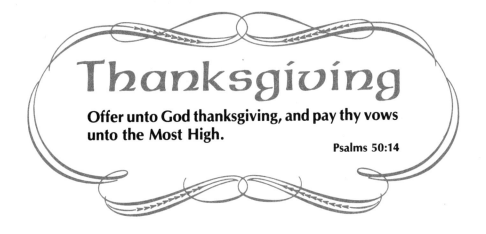

Thanksgiving

Offer unto God thanksgiving, and pay thy vows unto the Most High.

Psalms 50:14

I'll Thank Him Once Again

My God has done so much for me,
I never can repay,
That when I try to give Him thanks,
I know not what to say.
When I'm so low I cannot stand,
He makes my spirit soar,
For this I bow my lowly head
And thank Him just once more.

I thank Him for each drop of blood
He shed on Calvary's tree,
The crimson drops fell to the ground,
Oh, God, was that for me?
It was for me and every one
Who calls upon His name,
For this I bow my lowly head
And thank Him once again.

I dare not walk away from God
And His protecting power,
For He might call time to an end
And come at any hour.
And so I'll watch and wait for Him
Till time on earth shall end,
Then at His feet I'll bow my head,
And thank Him once again.

Dee Gaskin

Autumn Syndrome

Anne Coolidge looked from the window of her small, third floor apartment and thanked God for the view. She enjoyed sitting at the kitchen table that was pushed close to the window so she could sip her morning coffee and gaze down into the cramped next-door yard.

She never mentioned her pleasure to anyone because she felt that it wouldn't be considered much of a view. There was just an old rock maple standing in the center of a lawn that never grew lush-green even in the height of summer, a worn lilac bush that managed to cling to life in a sunless corner, and honeysuckle that thrived and even bloomed out rosy-pink loveliness in spite of lack of care. But to Anne, it was beauty, God's very breath, and she never tired of His wonders.

Now she did see a trace of loneliness in the yard and her eyes glistened. Not for herself but a leaf that she saw battered unmercifully by the wind. It was almost as if she were the leaf. "God grant you strength, little leaf," she whispered. "Hang on!"

Her fists even clenched, her muscles tensed, as if by so doing the dry leaf would vicariously receive her strength and energy.

The wind was victorious, though. Anne sighed, aware that she was being ridiculous relating to a dead leaf. Still, she sighed again and watched the leaf lose its hold and swirl away.

"Anne Coolidge," she declared, "the man in the white jacket will be after you!" But her heart disagreed and mourned the loss of a leaf she had been blessed to see bud, grow into a beautiful pattern of fresh, lacy green, transform into crimson red, then fade and shrivel.

"Oh, for one small patch of brightness," she murmured, yearning, wishing her neighbors had seen fit to grow small beds of marigolds and baby mums in their backyard.

She turned with a sigh, deciding to end this nonsense. But as she leaned over the table to gather the breakfast dishes, she caught a glimpse of brightness . . . a bird with an orange-red breast.

"A *robin!*" she cried. Her awe and delight couldn't have been greater if she had beheld a rare and exotic bird. "And I know why you're still here!" Happily, thankfully, she watched the colorful, chipper bird thrust out his red breast, hop about the drab yard, and cock his pretty head. *"There be a messenger with him . . ."* (Job 33:23), she whispered, silently thanking God. He had sent the bird to comfort and cheer the autumn heart. . . .

Clare Miseles

Thank You For Simple Things

An open Bible
  Sunrise—Sunset
    Dewy cobwebs on the grass
      Reflections mirrored in a pool
        A galaxy of stars mounted on blue velvet.

Shady nooks on a hot, sultry day
  The first robin and "peepers" of spring
    The wonder and fragrance of a perfect rose
      Kittens playing with a ball of yarn
        Freshly baked home-made bread.

Children's unaffected laughter
  Violets nestling in heart-shaped leaves
    Church bells on a Sunday morning
      The beauty and splendor of Autumn
        Buttered popcorn by the fire.

The song of the mocking bird
  A child kneeling in prayer
    A frisky puppy
      Snowy curtains gently blowing in the breeze
        Flashes of lightning.

Sparrows, strung like pearls upon a wire
  Frolicking baby lambs
    A harvest moon
      A winding brook
        Ermine coats on branch and twig.

Music and books and friends
  A startled deer darting out of sight
    A mother's hands
      A tree, heavy with fruit
        Memories—so many memories.

The clean, fresh smell of clothes from the line
  The sheen of polished wood
    A baby's toothless smile
      The young "wilds" of wood and fields.

Rhena S. LaFever

A Prayer At Summer's End

For fruit warm ripe in summer's sun,
For love and work and wholesome fun,
For raindrops on the windowpanes,
For walks down grassy country lanes,
For sunshine bright, for moonlight's glow,
For cornstalks marching, row on row,
For baby pigs, for laughter gay,
For fragrant smell of new-mown hay,
For food . . . and music . . . birdsongs sweet,
For restful, healing night time sleep,
For home with its familiar joys,
For carefree shouts of girls and boys,
For safe returns, for loving care,
For all the bliss of answered prayer,
For dancing stars, for firelight's gleam,
Fulfillment of a cherished dream,
For books and friends, a faith that sings,
For happiness homecoming brings,
For hope renewed, for courage born,
For breathless hush of early morn,
For this—a blessed interlude—
Dear God, accept my gratitude.

Ruby A. Jones

Autumn In The Hills

It's autumn in the hills again,
The leaves are bright as flame,
And with a pen of red and gold
October signs her name. . . .

A chirp, the southbound, winging birds,
In flocks light here and there,
To wish us well before they fly
Toward warmer planes somewhere.

What joy to share in harvesting,
Which burnished fields impart—
To store this golden autumn day
For memories in the heart!

Louise Weibert Sutton

Thanksgiving Day

Over the river and through the wood,
  To Grandfather's house we go;
    The horse knows the way
    To carry the sleigh
  Through the white and drifted snow.

Over the river and through the wood—
  Oh, how the wind does blow!
    It stings the toes
    And bites the nose,
  As over the ground we go.

Over the river and through the wood,
  Trot fast, my dapple-gray!
    Spring over the ground,
    Like a hunting hound!
  For this is Thanksgiving Day.

Over the river and through the wood,
  And straight through the barnyard gate.
    We seem to go
    Extremely slow—
  It is so hard to wait!

Over the river and through the wood—
  Now Grandmother's cap I spy!
    Hurrah for the fun!
    Is the pudding done?
  Hurrah for the pumpkin pie!

Julia Maria Child

GOLDEN THOUGHT

Autumn . . . the year's last, loveliest smile.

William Cullen Bryant

The Autumn Story

Much-thumbed,
The well-loved pages
Of softer sunlight and shadow;
The story
Written by an equinox wind
On leaves frost-etched in crimson
And gold.

E. Cole Ingle

October

Blond October comes striding over the hills wearing a crimson shirt and faded green trousers. His morning breath is the mist in the valleys, and at evening there are stars in his eyes, a waxing moon over his shoulder, and the cool whisper of valley breeze in his voice. He comes this way to light the fires of autumn in the maple groves, to put a final polish on the late winesaps, to whistle a farewell to summer and set the foxes to barking and tell the owls that now they can ask their eternal questions.

Now come the perfect days to get out and wander the hills and valleys of these latitudes. The scene changes from day to day, as though all the color in the spectrum were being spilled across the landscape—radiant blue of the sky and the lakes and ponds reflecting it, green of every tone in the conifers and in the reluctant oaks, yellows verging from "sun simmer" to "moon orange" in the elms, the beeches, the maples, and reds that range to purplish browns, sumac and dogwood and maple and oak and sour gum and sassafras and viburnum. There is the indigo of fox grapes, if you know where to find them.

October is colorful, it is exuberant, it is full of lively spirit. Spring fever can't hold a candle to October fever, when it comes to inner restlessness. The birds are on the wing, the leaves are footloose and eager for a breeze, the horizon is a challenge that amounts to an insidious summons. Listen closely and you can hear October, that fellow in the crimson shirt, whistling a soft melody that is as old as autumn upon this earth.

Hal Borland

November

November is all mist and mystery,
A month of undertones and muted greys,
When secret dreams become reality
And wonder walks down curving woodland ways.
It is a pause before the shawl of snow
Has silenced insects, turned the nights as still
As idle moments summer lovers know,
Who drowse in clover on a sun-warmed hill.
The hurrying is over and the year
Slopes gently down to comfortable sleep.
Indoors the fire of applewood flames clear,
As days close in and nights grow dark and deep.
Softly in this mist-shrouded interval
We hear time play the year's recessional.

Alice Mackenzie Swaim

A New Thanksgiving

They made a joyous feast of what they had
On that first long-ago Thanksgiving Day.
Looking not back with longing for a homeland far away,
For absent loved ones, better times, or more familiar fare—
Claiming an alien race as neighbors, brothers all,
They sat at meat with these, gladly to share
What was at hand. Singing their psalms of praise,
Facing with faith the uncertain future days.

Oh, these were men and women who stood tall,
Firm in their faith in God, strong, self-reliant, free—
These pioneers who dreamed high,
    worked hard, prayed unremittingly,
Built toward a nation with equality for all:
For all men, justice, dignity and liberty.

With such a heritage, can we do less?
Dare we with faith and courage face *our* wilderness?

We are Americans! We can do what we must:
Proudly proclaim again, "In God We Trust!"
Thank God for new dreams, new ways of living.
Thank God for this new Day of Thanksgiving!

B. L. Wolfe

Corn-Husking Time

Oh, the good old days of autumn,
　　Are the dearest of the year,
When the frost is on the pumpkin,
　　And the cider time is here.
When the hulls of juicy chestnuts
　　All the floors and hearth adorn,
Then we're in the prime of season,
　　And it's time to husk the corn.

As the smoke curls up the chimney
　　From the big, old-fashioned hearth,
There's a merry laughter ringing,
　　Which spreads sunshine o'er the earth.
There's an ecstasy in autumn,
　　On a bright and crispy morn,
When we take a shock of fodder
　　And begin to husk the corn.

There's no use for explanation
　　'Bout the joys both large and small,
As we leave the swelt'ring summer,
　　And we enter into fall.
There's a pleasure mixed with toiling,
　　On October's chilly morn,
And a rapture that is thrilling,
　　In the husking of the corn.

Tessa Webb

Thanks For Daily Bread

The best things are nearest: breath in your nostrils, light in your eyes, flowers at your feet, duties at your hand, the path of Right just before you. Then do not grasp at the stars, but do life's plain, common work as it comes, certain that daily duties and daily bread are the sweetest things of life.

Robert Louis Stevenson

The Old Barn

Weather-worn, the old barn stood
  on the brow of a gentle hill,
A sturdy relic of the past,
  in memory I see it still . . .
Its wide doors opened to a view
  of pastures lush and green
Where cattle grazed
  and quenched their thirst
  from a brook with water clean.

Swallows darted in and out;
  doves nested on its beams;
We played upon the scented hay
  and had our childhood dreams.
Happy days that old barn saw,
  those days that used to be,
Returning now, from out the past
  in pleasant memory.

Ernest Jack Sharpe

American Barns

Barns have always been an avenue of self-expression for the farmer. They have satisfied his yearning for beauty and his desire to project himself into the material things around him. The best American barns combine a harmonious blending of beauty and utility found nowhere else in the world of rural building design. Like every form of art, barn architecture grew; it did not spring full-blown from the brain of some carpenter, but, little by little, evolved from simple beginnings to the masterpieces which still stand as monuments to the creative ability of unlettered country craftsmen.

R. J. McGinnis

How The Pilgrims Built Their Towne

It was mid-December, 1620, when the "Mayflower" weighed anchor and sailed across Cape Cod Bay. When she came within six miles of the mainland, the wind changed and she had to beat out to sea again.

Next day, because the wind was fair, she came into Plymouth Harbor and anchored about a mile and a half offshore. Because of the shallow water, she could get no nearer. The passengers had to ferry from ship to shore through the stormy waters all winter long.

They made their decision to settle in this place by vote in the democratic way. Here by the abundant bay, at long last they would build. This would be their home and haven of rest after many storm-blown wanderings.

Between the sinister forests and the bay they would build a New England with their naked hands and a few tools, with sweat and tears and heartache.

Before starting to build, they planned well. The congregation was separated into nineteen families. Then along a street that led from the hill to the water's edge, the hill slope was divided into plots. The families drew lots for their location. John Carver, who had been their leader aboard the "Mayflower," was confirmed as governor for the coming year.

Twenty men remained ashore in a barricaded camp and began cutting timber for building. On Christmas Day they worked on the common house, or shelter, which was for storing provisions, ammunition, and clothing. All that day the axes swung. At night the weary builders went back to the ship, leaving twenty men ashore. Between decks on the "Mayflower" they ate a meager dinner with English cheer. Then they sang the old carols, with their hearts back again in merry England, as a storm lashed through the rigging of the "Mayflower" in Plymouth Harbor.

As the winter wore on, hacking coughs and fever and scurvy began to take their toll among the passengers. But whenever the rain and sleet died down, the men who could walk at all went ashore to work on the common house. They began the platform of the fort and the family dwellings along the new street.

When the common house was thatched, provisions and ammunitions were brought ashore and stored in it. In the remaining space the sick beds lay end to end. Here among the stricken lay Bradford and Carver.

One day a spark caught in the dry thatch of the common house, and its roof took fire. At the cries of alarm, the workmen rushed to the burning building and carried out the sick. Before the fire was checked, food and stores were damaged, but no lives were lost.

From the top of the mount, Miles Standish gazed grimly across the pine-clad hills in the west to where columns of smoke rose against the gray sky from Indian signal fires.

For this thing called freedom, Standish now well knew, there was a price to pay. Below him in the village, death had taken nearly half of the people. Rose Standish, his wife, was among the first who had died. He had knelt at her side at the last hour. He would rather have taken an arrow through his heart. Fourteen of the eighteen Pilgrim wives had died. They had been buried at night in unmarked graves, so that the savages should not know how few remained. Sometimes there were two or three deaths in a day.

He and a half dozen others still had strength enough to feed the thin soup to the sick, to cheer the wasted forms in the crude beds, to hew wood and carry water so that Plymouth might live.

Bradford from his sick-bed had watched the stocky man of war, day and night on his rounds, tending the sick with a woman's tenderness. Years later, rugged old Governor Bradford remembered and wrote this tribute in his blunt prose.

"There was but 6 or 7 sound persons, so to their great comendations be it spoken, spared no pains, night or day, but with abundance of toyle and hazard of their owne health, fetched them woode, made them fires, drest them meat, made their beads, washed their lothsome cloaths, cloathed and uncloathed them; in a word did all ye homly and necessarie offices for them which dainty and quesie stomacks can not endure to hear named; and all this willingly and cherfully, without any grudging in ye least, shewing herein their true love unto their friends and brethern. A rare example and worthy to be remembered. Tow of these 7 were Mr. William Brewster, ther Reverend Elder and Miles Standish ther Captein and military commander, unto whom myself and many others, were much holden in our low and sicke condition."

Death had come aboard the "Mayflower." The sickness took one by one the riotous crew who brutally ignored their comrades dying miserably in their bunks. To these men who had cursed and tormented them, the women aboard the ship brought what care and comfort they could with a Christlike compassion.

In the fires and ice of that first winter, their spirits were steel tempered to build a nation of men and women who would never turn back in quest of freedom and justice and of brotherhood.

James Daugherty

My Thanksgiving Prayer

My heart o'erflows with praise, dear Lord,
    For the wonders in our land;
The march of seasons, ocean tides,
    Directed by Thy Hand;
The golden dawns that signal day,
    And warmth of rising sun,
The star-lined canopies of night
    That fall when day is done;
The grandeur of the mountains crowned
    With opalescent snow,
The peaceful valleys scented sweet
    Where fruit and flowers grow;
The quiet streams where restless ones
    Relax and dream awhile,
The trees that offer shade and peace
    Along each leafy aisle;
My heart o'erflows with praise, dear Lord,
    And I offer thankful prayer
For the beauties on this planet earth
    I've been privileged to share.

Dorothy M. Cahoon

Our Thanks To God

Oh God, we give all thanks to Thee!
Thy presence, always near,
Is wondrously declared each day;
Thy hand has crowned this year
With goodness and the little hills
Rejoice on every side,
Though shadows loom, Thy voice instills
The peace in which we hide.
There is a refuge in the bough
For every bird that sings:
The valleys know a joy, for Thou
Hast sent unto them springs.
Thy strength hath set the mountain fast
And holds a restless sea,
Creator God, the First and Last—
Our thanks eternally!

Esther B. Heins

Pilgrim Mother Speaks

Mercy, help thy brother, child.
Bring wood for the hearth's bright blaze,
And heed thee that thee do not tip
That bowl of sun-dried maize.
Patience, stir the bubbling broth,
Take care with the heavy ladle,
And when thee has stirred the pot
Rock the baby's cradle.

Prudence, benches thee must dust,
And scrub the table board,
For tomorrow we will give
Our thanks unto the Lord.
All must be in readiness,
So be not idle, nor at play,
For hands and hearts and thoughts all make
A glad Thanksgiving Day.

Solveig Paulson Russell

The Meaning Of Thanksgiving

Once I was asked to speak to a group of elementary school children on the meaning of Thanksgiving. Afterwards, I asked that each child write letters to those persons to whom all of us should be grateful—individuals who ordinarily receive neither recognition nor expressions of gratitude.

The idea caught fire in the receptive minds of the children. They wrote hundreds of letters, expressing their thanks to the milkman, the paper boy, the postman, the garbage man, the traffic policeman near the school, and to their parents and teachers. The letters were warm and sincere, and they brought joy to both the senders and the receivers.

All of us can pause long enough to write letters of genuine appreciation to persons who need our attention, recognition and words of gratitude—to those who have been real blessings to us.

Through prayer we can also "write letters of gratitude" to God. He never tires of loving us and providing for our needs.

William Arthur Ward

Timmy Turkey's Thanksgiving

Young Timmy Turkey, on Thanksgiving Day,
Started out early to run far away.
Timmy lived on Hill Top Farm, but he was not happy. On the day before Thanksgiving, he had heard the children talking about the Thanksgiving feast they were to have. He overheard them say something about roast turkey and dressing. He was sure they were planning to have him for Thanksgiving dinner!

Tim said, "I will leave my home on the farm
And find one that's free from danger and harm."
He started down the road and across the fields. He walked as fast as he could, and once in a while he looked back to see if anyone was following him.

By night time he came to a deep, deep wood,
And under a tall, tall green tree he stood.
"Here in the deep woods I'll be safe," he said. "They'll never find me here. I'll never go back to the farm."

He wondered what was the best thing to do,
As to the branch of the big tree he flew.
Finally, he settled down on the branch for the night and tried to go to sleep, but it was hard to sleep in this strange place.

In the dark of night he heard a loud cry
From the brown branch of a high tree close by.
Timmy was frightened. He tried to stay still on his branch and did not move.

A voice seemed to say, "Whoo-whoo! Whoo-whoo-whoo!"
The turkey then wondered just what to do.
He heard the voice again saying, "Whoo-whoo?" Who could it be? How could anyone know he was hiding in the tree?

At last he answered and then told his name,
And he told the old owl just how he came
To be there in the deep, dark wood at night,
And why the voice gave him such a bad fright.
The owl listened as Timmy told of his home on the farm and that he had run away because he was afraid.

Then said Timmy Turkey, "What shall I do?
I can't always live in trees here with you."
Timmy's voice seemed to tremble as he went on to tell of his fears.

"My home is the farm not so far away,
But if I were there I'd be roast today."
The old owl turned his head to the right, and then he turned his head to the left. He ruffled his feathers and motioned for Timmy to be quiet so he could think.

The old owl pondered and thought what to do;
At last he said that he certainly knew.
He flapped his wings in his excitement and nodded his head up and down. Then he told Timmy just what to do. "You can't run away from your fears," he said. "You are still afraid here in the woods. You should have stayed on the farm where your friends loved you."

"Just walk down the road and go home today;
Thanksgiving is over—'twas yesterday."
Timmy could hardly wait until it was light to start for home. "I'll never run away again," he said. All of his friends and the children rushed to see him when he walked into the barnyard.

"Timmy, we missed you," they said. "We are so glad you are back!"

Timmy felt ashamed that he had run away because he was afraid. He lowered his head before he spoke.

"Listen and learn a good lesson from me;
Your home is the best place of all to be."

Nella Walters

Thankful

Thankful—for another day
       hours in which to work and play

Thankful—I can feel the sun,
       have good legs to walk and run

Thankful—I can smell the flowers,
       and while away some happy hours

Thankful—I can see God's beauty,
       while I rest or do some duty

Thankful—I can hear birds sing—
       Just "Thank You, God" for everything.

Nedra L. Krider

Autumn

Autumn wears an amber gown
Of taffeta and lace,
That rustles like the dying leaves
She forces out of place.

Linda Lowe

Something There Is About
A Bird's Nest

See what lies here
  midst the debris
  of autumn leaf, fungi,
  and wild berries,
  black and dry!

A bird's nest.

Something there is about a bird's nest
  that is holy,
    for it was built for eggs,
    and a mother nesting,
  and it became a home,
    when the eggs hatched out,
      for bird babies,
      until they were grown.

We could carry it back with us,
  but a nest doesn't belong
    inside.

A nest belongs to the woodlands,
  like the bird
    and the wild bird song.

So let us leave it here, where it fell.

Brown pine needles dropping into it,
  and autumn leaves blowing,
  will soon cover it over,
    and then the snow,
      white,
      and light . . .

Noemi Weygant

Friendship

Thou shalt love thy neighbor as thyself.
Matthew 22:39

The Worth Of A Friend

Can you measure the worth of a sunbeam,
The worth of a treasured smile,
The value of love and of giving
The things that make life worthwhile?
Can you cling to a precious minute
When at last it has ticked away?
At the end of a fleeting lifetime
Who of us dares bid it stay.

Can you measure the worth of tomorrow,
The good that by chance might come;
The heartaches, the joys and the sorrows,
Each an important one?
Life has a way of demanding
Right to the very end,
The prize to be sought . . . understanding,
That comes from the worth of a friend.

Can you measure the value of friendship,
Of knowing that someone is there;
Of faith and of hope and of courage,
A treasured and goodly share?
For nothing is higher in value,
Whatever life chooses to send . . .
We must prove that we, too, are worthy
And equal the worth of a friend.

Garnett Ann Schutlz

Mt. St. Helens and Spirit Lake, Washington

The Hymn That Makes The Whole World Kin

Many books have been written about the part hymns have played in promoting the spirit of Christian brotherhood. And most of them pay tribute to a hymn that was written nearly two hundred years ago in a parsonage in Yorkshire, England. As long as music remains an important part of Christian worship, "Blest Be the Tie That Binds" will arouse people to a deeper sense of human fellowship.

There is an intriguing story of how this hymn came to be written. Its author, the Reverend John Fawcett, was a Baptist pastor at Wainsgate, a village in Yorkshire. The forty-two-year-old parson was immensely popular in the community, but as so often happens, he found his salary of less than two hundred dollars a year hardly adequate for taking care of himself and his family.

But then came a call that seemed to solve his problem. In London, the noted preacher, Dr. Gill, was retiring, and the Wainsgate pastor was invited to take over that important pulpit. Without hesitation John Fawcett decided to accept the new position.

At last came the day in 1782, when he and his family were set to move. On the parsonage lawn were piled the minister's furniture and books; soon these would be loaded into wagons, and the long drive to London would begin.

But in that hour of farewell the Fawcett family were not alone. Grouped all around them in the most melancholy mood were the men, women, and children of the Wainsgate congregation. Their grief at parting with their beloved pastor was so keen that many were in tears.

Even as the pastor's family waited for the loading of their belongings, many pleaded with John Fawcett not to leave them.

As she sat on a packing case, hearing those earnest pleas, Mrs. Fawcett burst into tears.

"John," she exclaimed, "this is too much to bear. I do not want to leave this place."

"Nor I, my dear," her husband replied. "We'll stay where there are so many loving hearts, and continue our labors for the Lord here!"

And so, amid the cheers of the townspeople, the minister's things were carried back into the house. John Fawcett settled down in that pastorate where he spent the rest of his days.

It is said that his famous hymn "Blest Be the Tie That Binds" was written only a week after that touching scene on the parsonage lawn. No more appropriate words could have been composed to express the feeling of devotion and affection that had been shown toward this country pastor:

Blest be the tie that binds
  Our hearts in Christian love;
The fellowship of kindred minds
  Is like to that above.

Before our Father's throne
  We pour our ardent prayers;
Our fears, our hopes, our aims are one,
  Our comforts, and our cares.

We share our mutual woes,
  Our mutual burdens bear,
And often for each other flows
  The sympathizing tear.

When we asunder part,
  It gives us inward pain;
But we shall still be joined in heart
  And hope to meet again.

A hymn that has been sung in thousands of churches for nearly two centuries acquires a certain tradition. Probably no other song in the hymnal has come to stand for such warm Christian fellowship. At meetings of church workers the people present have been known on many occasions to break forth with "Blest Be the Tie That Binds," in an atmosphere of loving cooperation and understanding.

If ever there was a hymn that kindled in men's hearts the sincere fellowship and warmth of sympathy that the Christian faith has made possible throughout the whole wide world, Dr. Fawcett's stanzas have certainly achieved that purpose.

Vincent Edwards

Love

Joy is love exalted; peace is love in repose; long-suffering is love enduring; gentleness is love in society; goodness is love in action; faith is love on the battlefield; meekness is love in school; and temperance is love in training.

Dwight L. Moody

What Is Charity

It is Silence—when your words would hurt.
It is Patience—when your neighbor's curt.
It is Deafness—when a scandal flows,
It is Thoughtfulness—for others' woes.
It is Promptness—when stern duty calls,
It is Courage—when misfortune falls.

Author Unknown

Confide In A Friend

When you're tired and worn at the close of day
And things just don't seem to be going your way,
When even your patience has come to an end,
Try taking time out and confide in a friend.

Author Unknown

Departed Friend

I will place flowers on your
        grave
and what remains of your body
        but,
I will not accept your non-being.
        Because
You have not left. You never will.
        You
left me so many memories
        of
what you believed in,
        cried about,
        laughed at,
        experienced and
        said.
Now these are a precious part of me
I will transmit these to those I know,
    but who never knew you in life;
Then they will know you
        through me—
            by
what you left to me.

Wanda Kirby Gardner

golden thought

When we cannot find contentment in ourselves, it is useless to seek it elsewhere.

Ann Landers

If You Had A Friend

If you had a friend strong, simple, true,
Who knew your faults and who understood;
Who believed in the very best of you,
And who cared for you as a father would;

If you had a friend like this, I say,
So sweet and tender, so strong and true
You'd try to please him in every way
And live at your bravest, now wouldn't you?

His worth would shine in the words you praised
You'd shout his praises—yet—now how odd?
You tell me you haven't got such a friend
You haven't?—I wonder—*What of God?*

Robert Lewis

Martin Of Tours

"Truly, I say to you, as you did it to one of the least of these my brethren, you did it to me."

Matthew 25:40

Martin of Tours was a Roman soldier who became a Christian. One day he entered a city and was approached by a beggar. The feeble man was shivering and blue from the cold, and he held out his hand, hoping for some money. The Christian soldier had no money to give, but feeling sorry for the man, he took off his worn coat and cut it in half with his sword. He gave one half to the beggar and went on his way feeling that neither would freeze.

That night Martin had the often-recounted dream. He dreamed he saw angels, and Jesus was standing in the midst of them. Jesus was wearing half of a Roman soldier's coat. One of the angels asked, "Master, why are you wearing that tattered old rag?" Jesus answered, "My servant, Martin, gave it to me."

PRAYER: Our Father, help us to remember that in helping those less fortunate we are rendering a service to our Lord. Amen.

Lillus Mace

The Rose Bush

There were mixed feelings as all of the children and grand-children gathered around Granny Bates' bed. To me, she had always been old, wrinkled, white-haired.

We all wondered how much longer she could hold out, even with that amazing spunk that was a part of her.

She had a "last will and testament," and she constantly made us aware of it. Even now, in the last days of her illness, she requested that we all gather around her, and in a hoarse whisper, she said the last few words some of us would ever hear.

"My will shall take care of all of you," she said. "Be happy." And that is all I remember her saying.

We all gathered for the funeral. The room at the mortuary was banked with flowers and overflowed with people, mostly kinfolk. Cousin Vera sang, "Nearer My God to Thee" which Granny had requested. Preacher Jones gave the eulogy, then we accompanied Granny to her last resting place.

The will-reading was delayed until Lawyer Evans got back from his hunting trip where he couldn't be reached by phone.

The will dealt with us alphabetically so none would think Granny had shown partiality. Annie Mae and her family got the-South-Forty; Bobby and his wife, the house; Callie, the car and some bonds; Dennis, the livestock; Edward, the farm machinery; Fannie Lou, some cash money to help her go to college; Gerald, an insurance policy worth $1,000; Harvey and Ira, the same. I wasn't surprised that she left me the family picture album and her sewing machine, plus some knick-knacks which I prized, but I think all of us were taken aback when Mama's name was called out and all she got was a potted rose bush, a Peace Rose, at that.

"And to my daughter, Justina, I give my favorite flower. Of all my family, she has been the most faithful in nursing and caring for me. Because of this I bequeath her peace and happiness."

There was a simultaneous gasp from everyone, then a moment of absolute silence before we all began to tell her how sorry we were that we got things of value while Mama was left without.

"You can challenge the will," the lawyer suggested. "After all, your mother was well along in years and the court would take that into consideration. Then too, you did the most for her. You really should be recompensed for your efforts."

Mama shook her head and smiled what I then thought was a brave and courageous smile, belying what were probably her true feelings. I put my arm around her as though I might somehow give her strength.

"No," she said quietly, "Mama knew what she was doing. She had a reason for each of the legacies. I shall treasure the rose bush and think of her each time it blooms."

We drove out to Granny's house and picked up the rose bush and the two bushel baskets of old salad dressing bottles that she had given Mama, although I couldn't imagine what for.

As we were loading the plant and bottles into the car, we heard the voice of Granny's neighbor calling from the porch next door. It was Ben Acres, long retired because of poor hearing and eyesight. He wasn't at the funeral, with no way to get there on his own.

"Sorry to hear about Granny," he called. "I'll miss her!" I thought I saw a tear trickle down his leathery cheeks. Mama hesitated for a moment, then quickly broke off a rose and pushed the end of the stem into one of the bottles.

"Thank you, Ben," she said, handing him the blossom.

"The Peace," he replied, "I can't see it too well, but there is something about the way Granny's roses smelled that I'd know 'em anywhere."

Mama cared for that rosebush like it was Granny herself. She fed and watered it. Once I even caught her talking to it. And that bush responded with blooms all year.

Mama was always giving roses away. One time to a sick person; another time to say "thank you" to someone. Yet, there were always blossoms left to give.

Eventually I finished school and then married. I hated to leave Mama, but I had to go where my husband's work was.

"Your place is with your husband," Mama told me with a smile and a hug. We wrote back and forth once a week. Her letters always told about how one of the roses made someone happy.

Then one day, I received a letter from her asking for our prayers. Seems like one year, long ago, the taxes didn't get recorded, and the books showed that Mama owed about four hundred dollars in back taxes. Somebody from out-of-town had paid the taxes and claimed the house for himself. It was perfectly legal, the judge said.

The sheriff came and set her belongings out in the street. Poor Mama! She didn't know what to do. The rest of the family didn't seem to be concerned, the few that were left in the county. But word got around. The whole town was aroused.

"You brought me flowers when I was sick," said some. "Come and stay with us."

"You sent a rose when my baby was born," said another. "I'll share my food with you."

"I was depressed and wondered if life was worth living," said a

Continued on page 116

Continued from page 115

neighbor, "then you brought me a rose in a salad dressing bottle and I was reassured."

One by one the townspeople came with their testimonials and offers of help. A collection was taken up to buy back the house, and some of the men talked with the man who had bought the house.

I was expecting my baby any day now, so the doctor told me not to travel. I kept in touch by phone and was overjoyed to hear that the town had called a special day for celebration: "Justina Day."

The men built a platform in the middle of the downtown square. The women got together a kitchen band, and others helped cook for the crowd. People came from miles around, and enough money was raised to buy the house back, pay the taxes, and put a tidy sum in the bank so Mama wouldn't have to work so hard anymore.

My baby was born conveniently enough so I could attend the celebration. I looked around at the neighborhood, taking in all the familiar sights of my youth, and there in the middle of our front yard was the Peace Rose blooming its fool head off.

I remembered Granny's will and marveled at the foresight she had shown. The other members of the family had gone through their gifts from Granny. Some had wasted, others had spent, but it seemed that with Mama's rose bush the more she gave away, the more came back to her in one way or another. It just seemed right to her to share the beautiful roses with folks who needed them.

Ida M. Clark

Gift Of A Rose

I plucked a rose, a crimson rose,
Washed clean with summer rain
And gave it with a prayer to one
Whose hours were gray with pain.
And when I left the little room,
A fragrance warm and sweet
Was my companion as I walked
Along the quiet street.
For oh, a fragrance sweeter far
Than any wind that blows
Through summer gardens lingers on
The hand that gives a rose.

Grace V. Watkins

golden nugget

I have met people so empty of joy, that when I clasped their frosty finger tips it seemed as if I were shaking hands with a northeast storm. Others there are whose hands have sunbeams in them, so that their grasp warms my heart. It may be only the clinging touch of a child's hand; but there is as much potential sunshine in it for me as there is in a loving glance for others.

Helen Keller

WHAT MAKES FRIENDSHIP HAPPEN?

What makes friendships happen?
Is it accident or design?
What made this special feeling
Start between your heart and mine?

What special words did we exchange?
Perhaps we'll never know.
Or was it during the quiet hours
The warmth began to grow?

I like to think our Father knew
You needed me as I needed you
And that the friendship our hearts share
Is ours because He put it there.

Just want to say how glad I am,
From one day to another,
That somehow in God's special plan
We happened to each other!

Jean Kyler McManus

Dr. Paul Mansfield, Office Upstairs

His name was Paul Mansfield. When he graduated from medical school his professors predicted he would become one of the greatest surgeons of the world. They were right—but they didn't know just how right they were. His commitment to the Lord at an early age had already determined his course of action.

After graduation he turned down a partnership with a distinguished physician and moved to a desolate little village in the coal mining region of Appalachia. The only doctor in a 50-mile radius, he opened a small office in a room over the town's one dry goods store. For 40 years he ministered to the poor, living and working out of his office above the store.

He delivered babies in hovels where even the animals shivered in the cold. He extracted tonsils, set broken limbs, and sutured cuts—even without the aid of basic drugs. He diagnosed disease, performed minor operations, and referred, when necessary, to the big city hospital 50 miles away. He helped the aged, comforted the incurables, tended the dying and suffered through many a long, cold night with anxious loved ones.

Everyone was poor. Very poor. They paid him as they could, sometimes in produce, but most of the time not at all. But he was not working for a wage, because he had received a "calling" to minister. His goal: to heal the sick.

When the flu epidemic struck the mountain area, he gave himself day after day—traveling from one mountain shack to another giving shots and antibodies. There was little time for sleep for as soon as he lay his weary head on the pillow in his upstairs office there would be a knock at the door or the phone would ring. It wasn't long before he, too, became a victim of the flu.

His last conscious act was to call for his day book and across each account scribble "Paid in Full." Then he died.

People came from all over the mountains to attend his funeral. They even shut down the operations in the coal mines so the men could pay homage. The little white church was jammed with people. They stood outside the windows, the women in bonnets and

the men holding little children on their shoulders—most of whom had been delivered by the country doctor.

Eight strong mountain men, looking strange in their mismatched coats and ties, carried the casket from the church. Placing it on their shoulders they walked quietly down the mountain path to the country graveyard. Hundreds of people fell in step behind them, singing softly with tear-stained faces, "There's a land that is fairer than day . . . and by faith we shall see it afar . . ."

They lowered the wooden box into the open grave, and then by common consent scattered far and wide. Each person returned with a stone which he placed on the grave. The mountain of rocks was shoulder high when the last stone was in place.

Then the country preacher stepped forward and laid the last object on the grave. It was the doctor's shingle that he had pulled off the pole in front of the dry goods store. It simply said, "Dr. Paul Mansfield; Office Upstairs."

Jamie Buckingham

GOLDEN THOUGHTS

Who pleasure gives, shall joy receive.

Benjamin Franklin

The true measure of a man is how he treats someone who can do him absolutely no good.

Rochefoucauld

True friends have no solitary joy or sorrow.

Channing

A pleasant possession is useless without a friend.

Seneca

I would not live without the love of my friends.

Keats

The ornaments of our house are the friends that frequent it.

Ralph Waldo Emerson

Because I Love You

Because I love you I can look at life
   with clearer eyes,
And face tomorrow with a braver heart,
And hold my chin up with a brand new hope,
And know that I must finish things I start.

Because I love you I've become more kind
And gentle with my friends from day to day,
For watching you, your attitude of life,
Has taught me more than words could
   ever say.

And this you did without a word, a touch,
Perhaps your heart will never ever know;
But when you drop a pebble in a pond,
You never know how far the ripples go.

Because I love you, everything's become
More beautiful as seasons come and go,
I can reach up and touch the heart of God,
Because, oh yes . . . because I love you so!

Grace E. Easley

Putting Back The Stars

May friends remember me
As one who with his light
Lit every lamp he saw
While stumbling through this night;
As one who gladly did
A thousand thankless chores
'Til those shut out from love
Could pass through long-locked doors.
May friends remember me
And say of my replies,
"His words put back the stars
In our dark, faithless skies."

Perry Tanksley

The Lion And The Mouse

Once upon a summer's day
A little mouse went out to play.
He slid down hills of slippery moss
And chased balloons of milkweed floss.
Some acorns lying on the ground
Made dandy balls to kick around.
He kicked them through a clump of weeds,
And there he found some crunchy seeds.

"Good!" he cried, "I'll have a feast!"
Just then he spied a huge wild beast,
A lion, napping 'neath a tree!
The little mouse said, "Lucky me!
Here's a lion fast asleep.
I'll climb upon his back and creep
Into his long and shaggy hair.
It should feel nice and tickly there."

The little mouse began to climb.
Alas, in hardly any time
The lion wakened from his doze
And grabbed the mouse's four front toes.
The lion roared, "You little pest!
How dare you interrupt my rest!
I'll swat you hard, that's what I'll do.
And that will be the end of you!"

The mouse cried, "I apologize.
It was foolish, most unwise,
To ever creep into your mane.
I'll never try that trick again.
Please spare my life. Oh, won't you please?
I beg you, sir, on bended knees.
If you do, I have no doubt
That some day I can help you out."

The lion laughed and slapped his side.
He laughed until he almost cried.
He caught his breath and then he spoke,
"A *mouse* help *me*? Oh what a joke!

How could such a tiny thing
Help me out, the mighty king
Of all the beasts that roam the earth?
Begone, before I choke with mirth!"

The mouse ran off most gratefully,
Still alive, unharmed, and free.
"Thanks," he said, "I still intend
To help you when I can, kind friend."
The lion winked a merry eye,
And chuckled as he waved good-bye.

The days flew by, and then one morning,
The lion, without word of warning,
Fell into a hunter's snare.
His mighty roaring pierced the air.
Some hunters came and smiled with glee.
They tied him tightly to a tree,
Then ran to find a cart or dray
To haul the captured beast away.

The lion roared and kicked and thrashed.
He snarled and snorted, growled and gnashed.
He pulled and strained with all his might;
The hunter's knots were very tight.
He could not loosen up the rope.
Then just as he was losing hope,
A little voice said, "Have no fear,
You needn't worry now *I'm* here."

The tiny mouse waved his paw.
He wasn't strong but he could gnaw.
He found the rope, crept underneath,
Then gnawed it with his sharp mouse teeth.
The mouse worked hard and he worked fast,
And set the lion free at last!

The big cat stretched and shook his head,
"I thank you, little friend," he said.
"You helped me as you said you would,
I never really thought you could."
The mouse said, "Now you realize
One cannot judge friends by their size.
On friendship each of us depends,
And often small folks make great friends."

Frances B. Watts

Moments Of Gold

Two or three minutes—two or three hours—
What do they mean in this life of ours?
Not very much
If but counted as time;
But moments of gold
And hours sublime,
If only we use them
Once in a while
To make someone happy—
To make someone smile.
A minute may dry
A little boy's tears.
An hour sweeps aside
The trouble of years.
Minutes of my time
May bring to an end
Hopelessness somewhere,
And bring me a friend.

Lucille Crumley

Ghost-Music Of A Rail Journey

By a window
Of a train
I remain
All alone

Empty platform
Early morning
And a whistle's
Lonely moan

(Was it here
Or was it there
Where she whispered
Her goodbye?

Is she coming?
Am I going?
Darkened hills
And vacant sky)

Yet ahead
A fire's burning
Slowly, slowly
Wheels are turning

Turning, turning,
Turning, turning
Journey's start
And no returning

By a window
Of a train
I remain
All alone.

A. V. Riasanovsky

Worship

Let the people praise thee, O God; let all the people praise thee.

Psalms 67:3

Great Faith That Smiles Is Born Of Great Trials

It's easy to say, *"In God we trust"*
When life is radiant and fair,
But the test of faith is only found
When there are burdens to bear—
For our claim to faith in the "sunshine"
Is really *no faith at all*
For when roads are smooth and days are bright
Our need for God is so small,
And no one discovers the fullness
Or the greatness of God's love
Unless he has walked in the "darkness"
With only a *light* from *Above*—
For the faith to endure whatever comes
Is born of sorrow and trials,
And strengthened only by discipline
And nutured by self-denials—
So be not disheartened by troubles,
For trials are the "building blocks"
On which to erect a *fortress* of *faith*
Secure on God's "ageless rocks."

Helen Steiner Rice

Understanding

The troubles that beset you
 Along life's winding road
Are sent to make you stronger
 To share another's load.

We cannot share a sorrow
 If we haven't grieved a while,
Nor can we feel another's joy
 Until we've learned to smile!

Sweet mystery of music,
 Great masters and their art,
How well we understand them
 When we've known a broken heart!

Let tyrants lust for power,
 Sophisticates be wise,
Just let me see the world, dear God,
 Through understanding eyes.

Nick Kenny

On A Rainy Day

Lord, help me to see the beauty in a day that is cloudy and dreary and wet. Somehow I tend to think that beauty goes hand in hand with sunshine, but help me realize that the beauty lies in the fact that I can hear the rain as it falls on the bushes and trees—that I can feel the softness of the water on my skin—that I can see each tiny raindrop as it hangs so delicately from a leaf, or clings to a windowpane.

Help me to know that there cannot always be sunshine. Rain is needed for growth. So, in life, the showers come also. They, too, are needed to learn and grow and, after each shower the sun shines again. As the earth looks to you for sun and rain, may I look to you for wisdom and understanding.

Thank you for your blessings to me, and for your love, so beautifully shown in the strength of the sunlight and in the tenderness of a raindrop.

Marian Heck

The Link That Binds

Faith is the wondrous, living link
   That binds the trusting soul to God;
It lights the darkness, smooths the way,
   Gives comfort through His staff and rod.

Faith makes the past an open book;
   It trusts His word, yields to His power;
Lays hold of God's almighty hand,
   And lives with Him from hour to hour.

Faith proves His every promise sure;
   It feels the final triumph near;
It ever dwells with hope and love,
   And casts out every haunting fear.

Faith works by love the soul to cleanse;
   It purifies the heart and life;
It triumphs over every foe,
   Gives victory in daily strife.

Lord, give me such a faith as this,
   That firm my trust may be in Thee;
Help me to keep the narrow way,
   For I, in peace, Thy face would see.

C. P. Bollman

The Way Of Deliverance

Crisis brings us face to face with our own inadequacy and our own inadequacy in turn leads us to the inexhaustible sufficiency of God. This is the power of helplessness, a principle written into the fabric of life.

Catherine Marshall

The Missing Lamb

For years I was a shepherd. Oh sure, I was a business man, going to the office each day. But after-office hours and weekends were spent on my small farm on the outskirts of town.

Naturally I never *thought* of myself as a shepherd. The word just never occurred to me. The usual picture of a shepherd is a man in sagging garments, leaning forward with the wind. He carries a stout gnarled crook, or stick. His eyes are sunken in a bearded face, and shadowed with a strange cap.

I, in turn, was not exactly dressed by Brooks Brothers, but after arriving home I would pull on a pair of well-fitting dungarees and plaid flannel shirt, then go out and check on the lambs.

Every night, especially during the lambing season, I had to round up and count my flock of ten. The sheep had names, but the lambs were just numbers.

One cold autumn evening I counted, not to ninety and nine, but to eight and one. One of my lambs was missing!

It was almost dark. I must hurry. Where should I look first in all that pasture area? Why was I bothering, anyway, cold and hungry and bone weary?

I didn't know.

We had no mountains but we had hills. We were not menaced with wolves but we were plagued with stray dogs. My steps increased to a jog. Down Long Meadow. Now up behind Chimney Hill. There was no assuring sound. No welcome sight. Where was my lamb?

Finally, over in the back pasture where the grass runs out, a trap-laden mass of underbrush and brambles muffled a thin wavering cry. This spurred me on.

I located the source of the cry in a clutch of those painful "cat briars." There were a half-dozen crisscrossed strands with their long sharp talon-like thorns holding him painfully motionless. Yes, there he was, the little lost lamb caught in his waywardness and ignorance.

Happy that I had found my lost lamb, I stooped to untangle and free him from his bounds. As my two hands lifted him gently, the picture of another Shepherd flashed before me with impressive brilliance and clarity.

It was the well-known picture of The Good Shepherd in the famous scene where he stoops to rescue that other lost lamb. It was not a "vision." But it was a sudden mental connecting of the two scenes.

Why, then, did this mental picture affect me so strangely? Why was the impact so strong? Why was I standing so still warming the trembling lamb in my arms? Why this sudden burst of joy?

Yes. Yes, that was it. Now I knew. I, too, had been a lamb once lost. But, glory be, on another autumn evening a few years' past, I, too, had been assured of the peace that passes all understanding.

Again I realized that Christ was *my* Shepherd and Savior. I had been lost but I was found and safe in his fold, forever!

H. Ramsey Terhune

I Found Love

In a garden, I found contentment.
In a seed, I found faith.
In a flower, I found God.
In a tree, I found patience.

In a butterfly, I found beauty.
In a smile, I found acceptance.
In a touch, I found encouragement.
In a friend, I found joy.

In a child, I found trust.
In a parent, I found generosity.
In a storm, I found courage.
In a rainbow, I found hope.

In a sunset, I found serenity.
In a mountain, I found immortality.
In service, I found fulfillment.
In a book, I found truth.

In a teacher, I found wisdom.
In a prayer, I found peace.
In a song, I found freedom.
In You, I found love.

William Arthur Ward

I Pray

Let me be patient,
    If I would hurry—
Keep me silent,
    When I am angry.

Let me be humble,
    And do no wrong—
Make me be gentle,
    So I will be strong.

Let me thank Thee,
    Dear God, for this day—
Help me, and keep me,
    All my life, I pray.
             —Amen—

Florence H. Cottrill

The Flame

In my heart, a flame,
intense and unquenchable,
ah! Your holy Name!

Eleanor Di Giulio

True Religion

At home it is kindness.
In business it is honesty.
In society it is courtesy.
In work it is thoroughness.
In play it is fairness.
Toward the fortunate it is congratulations.
Toward the weak it is help.
Toward wickedness it is resistance.
Toward the penitent it is forgiveness.
Toward God it is reverence, love, and obedience.

Anonymous

Love Without End

When every mountain, lake and tree
Spread lovingly upon earth's face
Exemplifies divinity—
How can we doubt His boundless grace?

Jaye Giammarino

A Helping Hand

God has His hand in yours
In everything you do
So put your hand in His
And He will come to you.

Shirl

The Beautiful Hands Of Jesus

Hands beckoning disciples to follow—they knew not where.

Hands resting in blessing on the heads of little children or on deformed, disease-ridden bodies in the act of healing.

Hands calling back to life those who had fallen into eternal sleep.

Hands extended to offer comfort and solace to the confused and bewildered.

Hands that could shake with righteous indignation over the desecration of His Father's house, yet reach out in mercy and forgiveness to all who called upon Him.

Hands clasped in anguished prayer in the garden of Gethsemane.

Humble hands that washed the feet of His disciples and later broke the bread and passed the cup at the Last Supper.

Hands torn and bleeding on the Cross of Calvary.

Quiet hands folded in the tomb—too quiet hands!

Hands held out in greeting to those He loved following His resurrection.

Hands raised victoriously and triumphantly Heavenward on Ascension Day as He blest the world upon leaving it forever in the form of man.

Rhena S. LaFever

GOLDEN NUGGET

We can and should worship God in gratitude for what He has done for us, but it reaches a higher level when we worship Him simply for what He is, for the perfections and excellence of His own being.

J. Oswald Sanders

Evening Worship

I passed a little church at dusk,
But did not enter though I should.
Instead, I took a friendly path
That led me to a mystic wood.

So hushed the tall and ancient trees,
So sweet the night wind on my face,
I felt God's reassuring hand,
And knelt in worship at that place.

William Arnette Wofford

Green Cathedral

Under these arches
Of giant pine
This forest nave
This shrine,
Walk gently
To the music
Of a woodland spring
And wind blown leaves
That sing.

Stand quietly
And watch
A sunlit altar,
A stone,
Draped with smooth green moss
As a great oak
With arms outstretched
Reflects the shadow
Of a cross.

Joseph D. Tonkin

Church Bells

What do you hear when the church bells chime?
Do they arouse a conscience call
Or do they flood your heart with joy
Remembering God is over all?

What do you think when the bells ring out?
"I must go," (from a sense of duty)
Or, are you filled with happiness
That their message is one of beauty.

What is this message that the bells peal forth?
The Christian's reply is sure.
"It is love and hope and forgiveness too,
The world's no longer a lure."

What should we learn from our church bells?
As their sweet tones float through the air,
We are a part of the Kingdom of God
And in this we all have a share.

Our lives can be both chimes and bells,
Our message can spread like the dew,
But without God to make them ring
The notes are all too few.

Rhena S. LaFever

Family Album Favorite

"Jesus, It's Jim..."
"Jim, It's Jesus"

The preacher, a puzzled frown on his face, hurried to the cottage where the Church caretaker lived.

"I am worried," he explained. "Every day at 12 o'clock a shabby old man goes into the church. I can see him through the parsonage window. He only stays a few minutes. It seems most mysterious and you know the altar furnishings are quite valuable. I wish you would keep an eye open, and question the fellow."

The next day, and so for many days, the caretaker watched, and sure enough, at 12 o'clock the shabby figure would arrive.

One day the caretaker accosted him: "Look here, my friend, what are you up to, going into the church every day?"

"I go to pray," the old man replied quietly.

"Now come," the caretaker said sternly, "you don't stay long enough to pray. You are only there a few minutes, for I have watched you. You just go up to the altar every day and then come away."

"Yes, that's true. I cannot pray a long prayer, but every day at 12 o'clock I just come and say, 'Jesus, it's Jim.' Then I wait a minute, then come away. It's just a little prayer, but I guess He hears me."

Some time later poor old Jim was knocked down by a truck, and was taken to the city hospital where he settled down quite happily while his broken leg mended.

The ward where Jim lay had been a sore spot to the hospital nurses for a long time. Some of the men were cross and miserable, others did nothing but grumble from morning till night. Try as the nurses would, the men did not improve.

Then slowly but surely things changed. The men stopped grumbling and were cheerful and contented. They took their medicine, ate their food and settled down without a complaint.

One day, hearing a burst of happy laughter the nurse asked: "What has happened to you all! You are such a nice cheerful lot of patients now. Where have all the grumbles gone?" "Oh, it's old Jim," one patient replied. "He is always so happy, never complains although we know he must be in a lot of pain. He makes us ashamed to make a murmur. No, we can't complain when Jim's around, he's always so cheerful."

The nurse crossed over to where Jim lay. His silvery hair gave him an angelic look. His quiet eyes were full of peace. "Well, Jim," she greeted him, "the men say you are responsible for the change in this ward. They say you are always happy."

"Aye, Nurse, that I am. I can't help being happy. You see, Nurse, it's my visitor. Every day he makes me happy."

"Your visitor?" The nurse was puzzled. She had always noticed that Jim's chair was empty on visiting days, for he was a lonely old man without any relatives. "Your visitor," she repeated. "But when does he come?"

"Every day," Jim replied, the light in his eyes growing brighter. "Yes, every day at 12 o'clock. He comes and stands at the foot of my bed. I see Him, and He smiles and says, 'Jim, it's Jesus.'"

Author Unknown

The Voice Of God

GOD speaks to us in nature
Could we but know His voice
Each glowing, golden sunrise
Is reason to rejoice.

GOD speaks to us in nature
In the wind that sways the trees
In the hurricane and raindrops
In the gentlest little breeze.

GOD speaks to us in nature
In the feathered creature's song
In the rushing water's rhythm
In the earth it runs along.

GOD speaks to us in nature
In the mountains soaring high
In the brightness of the moonlight
In the star-bejeweled sky.

GOD speaks to us in nature
We must listen for His word
In the wind, the brook, the
Hilltops, rising run and trilling bird.

Kay Adele Leonard

My Lord And I

In the quiet midnight hours
When no sleep is in the eye,
I commune with Christ my Saviour
As the moments hurry by.

Oh! how precious are those moments
As I feel His presence near,
And a voice that seems to whisper
I am with thee, do not fear.

Just remember I have promised
That thy Refuge I will be,
When in trouble or in sorrow
I will comfort thee.

Fear thou not, for I am with thee,
'Tis written in the Book divine
I will strengthen and uphold thee
Only Trust Me, Child of Mine.

When thou passeth through the waters
And the river's deep and wide,
They shall not overflow thee
For I'll be at thy side.

So when the storms of life are ended,
And I rest beside the sea,
There I'll meet my Lord and Saviour
Who suffered all for me.

It was He who bore my burden
On the Cross of Calvary,
So I'll sing His praise forever
Throughout all Eternity.

Amelia J. Locke

Blessed Creation

God is,
> therefore the mighty
>> strength of the mountains.

God is,
> therefore the majestic
>> grandeur of the seas.

God is,
> therefore the luxuriant
>> wealth of the earth.

God is,
> therefore a wondrous
>> world of love.

God is,
> therefore I am.

Helen deLong Woodward

Roots

Let my roots grow deep into you, Lord,
> like trees by streams of water
> grow deep to find life-giving food
> to produce fruit in season:
> gentleness, faith, joy and love.

Let my roots grow deep into you, Lord,
> draw nourishment, love and power
> till every fiber of my being
> grows strong and life o'er flows
> with thanksgiving, joy and love.

Let my roots grow deep into you, Lord,
> down into the rich soil of your love
> drink freely the power of your spirit
> that my life may be verdant, giving shade—
> an oasis of hope, joy and love.

Let my roots grow deep into you, Lord,
> becoming vigorous and strong
> a ready shelter in life's storms
> for those who've lost their way
> to find in you: joy and love.

Leota Campbell

Let's Read It Together
the children's corner

Thoughts Of A Small Boy In Church

I wonder why I have to go
To church with Mom and Dad, you know
It seems so big, and I'm so small,
'N I can't see a thing at all
Except the high back of the pew
In front of me, and then a few
Backs of heads with funny hats,
Some high, some flowered, some like mats:
And when the folks stand up to sing,
That's when I can't see anything!
When I sit down my feet won't touch,
And if I swing 'em Mom says "Hush!"
"Can't you sit still? You'll drop that book!"
Then "Big Hat" turns with frowning look.
I don't think she likes little boys.
I try hard not to make a noise!

And then the preacher starts to talk.
O, how I'd like to take a walk!
His words are big, his voice booms out—
I don't know what it's all about.
I wish that church for little folks
Could be like in my story books.
The pictures Grandma shows to me
Have children close to Jesus' knee.
They're talking, laughing, sit or stand,
And some are holding His big hand.
He's talking to them tenderly.
Wish He could talk like that to me!

When I get big I'm going to build
A childrens' church and have it filled
With little chairs, have windows bright
That let in all God's lovely light—
And when it's warm they'll open wide
And let birds' songs come right inside,
'N smells of flowers God has made,
And not one child will be afraid

To laugh or sing or swing his feet,
Or reach out 'til his fingers meet
Another child's who'll be his friend.
They'll sweet tunes sing as voices blend
In songs of praise and songs of love
For this big world and God above.
They'll have a preacher who will know
A child likes voices soft and low.
He'll tell about his childhood days
And how he learned to love Christ's ways.
He'll let the children laugh and sing
And just be glad for everything!

Esther Bird Doliber

Wondering

You know I often wonder—
    When Jesus was a boy
Did He have a bright red wagon
    And a special bedtime toy?

Did He ever own a kitten
    Or a puppy dog to cuddle?
Did His mother ever scold Him
    When He waded in a puddle?

Oh, I hope He walked barefooted
    Through dewy grass in spring
To find the fallen feather
    From a downy bluebird's wing.

Perhaps He filled his pockets
    With pebbles, round and white
Or climbed a windy hilltop
    To fly a paper kite.

Do you think that He was happy
    As any boy should be?
Were there butterflies and tadpoles
    And frogs in Galilee?

I am certain that You watched Him
    Through His childhood play and fun;
For the sweet and gentle Jesus
    Was Your own dear precious Son!

Jean Conder Soule

Inspiration

I didn't do my chores today,
For somehow work seemed far away,
Instead I wandered down a lane,
And touched a flower, kissed with rain.

I sat beside a waterfall,
And heard a bluebird's mating call,
I touched the grass beneath my feet,
And smelled the flowers, soft and sweet.

I gazed at trees so tall and strong,
And watched the leaves that danced along,
I saw the clouds go drifting by,
As wild geese filled the spacious sky.

Oh yes, I took a rest today,
For somehow work seemed far away,
Tomorrow I'll work twice as hard,
But today I spent the day with God.

Patricia Ann Emme

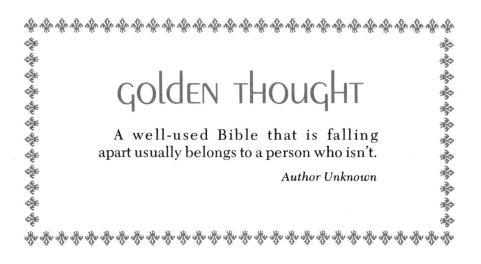

GOLDEN THOUGHT

A well-used Bible that is falling
apart usually belongs to a person who isn't.

Author Unknown

Chapel of Holy Cross, Sedona, Arizona

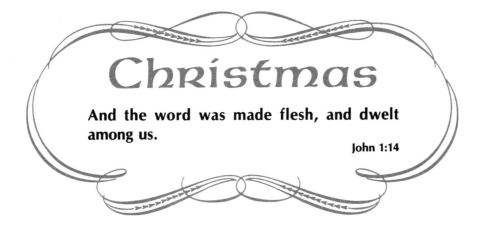

Christmas

And the word was made flesh, and dwelt among us.

John 1:14

Christmas

A soft lighted creche on your hearthstone,
A greeting from old friends afar,
The carolers' song at your doorstep,
The light of a bright treetop star.

Bright candlelights glowing in windows,
And hurrying throngs on the street,
A kind deed you've done for a stranger,
Whom, troubled, you happened to meet.

The mem'ry of happy child faces,
The sparkle of crusted snow-sheen,
And families gathered together,
Woodsy odors from cut evergreen.

A day set apart from all others,
An awesome hush touching the night,
The story of shepherds and wisemen
Who traveled by one bright star's light.

May the peace and the joy of the season
Fill your hearts as that first Christmas morn.
"Unto you a Saviour is given,
Lo, to you a Christchild is born."
That's Christmas!

Esther Bird Doliber

The Throng Passed By

This new baby,
Could he be
the hope of Israel,
the Savior promised?
Poor shepherds came
to worship him
but the throng passed by.

Joseph, a just man
and tender,
protected the child,
loved him
worked hard to provide,
but the throng passed by.

Mary magnified her God
with wonders in her heart,
praise on her lips
and mother-love
at its best,
but the throng passed by.

The poor shepherds
are now immortal,
Joseph remembered–
a just and kindly man,
Mary called blessed
by all generations,
but the throng passed by.

Leota Campbell

The Three Kings

What must have been their feelings when the star
Which they had followed from the distant East,
Loomed above a cavern in the hill,
The home, not of a king, but of the least
Of men—they had come to find a prince.
Monarchs dwell in palaces of gold
And marble, not in stables with an ox
Or ass, with only straw against the cold.

Their eyes were troubled and their hearts afraid.
Had their lengthy journey been in vain?
There was no mansion underneath the star,
And yet it was the signal to ordain
Where the King would be. Should they turn back
And look elsewhere, forget the dream, or go
Inside the cave and see what they would see.
Wrapping their cloaks about them, bending low
They entered in the stable door, and found
The Infant King enthroned on manger board
Bright with straw. Asking no questions they
Looked at Him, and falling down, adored.

Anne Tansey

Little Fires

The little fires that blaze on Christmas Eve
Are lit by simple folk whose hearts believe
The Christ Child wanders softly through the night
And blesses all who set a guiding light.
(O little Child, I tend my fires and pray,
For fires around the world to guide thy way.)

Dorothy Linney

Golden Scripture

For unto us a child is born, unto us a son is given; and the government shall be upon his shoulder; and his name shall be called Wonderful, Counsellor, Mighty God, Everlasting Father, Prince of Peace.

Isaiah 9:6

Unseen Gifts

There is nothing I can give you which you do not have, but there is much that while I cannot give it, you can take.

No Heaven can come to us unless our hearts find rest in it today. Take Heaven.

No Peace lies in our future which is not hidden in this present instant. Take Peace.

The gloom of the world is but a shadow, behind it, yet within reach is joy, there is radiance and glory in the darkness could we but see and to see we have only to look. I beseech you to look.

Life is so generous a giver, but we, judging its gifts by their covering, cast them away as ugly or heavy or hard. Remove the covering and you will find beneath a living splendor woven of love, by wisdom with power.

Welcome it, grasp it, and you touch the angel's hand that brings it to you. Everything we call a trial, a sorrow or a duty, the angel's hand is there, the gift is there and the wonder of an over-shadowing presence. Our joys too be not content with them as joys. They too conceal diviner gifts.

And so at this time I greet you, not quite as the world sends greetings, but with profound esteem and the prayer that for you, now and forever, the day breaks, the shadows flee away.

Fra Giovanni–1513

Holly In Your Heart

Traffic was heavy, and one taxi driver tangled his mudguard in another taxi's fender. One driver grew red in the face and let loose an incredible stream of invectives upon the other driver.

The latter bore it patiently as long as he could. Then, holding up his hand, he pointed to the little sprig of holly adorning his rival's radiator cap. "'Ere, mate, give over, carn't yer?" he said in injured tones. "What's the good of 'aving 'olly on yer bonnet if your ain't 'olly in yer 'eart?"

Author Unknown

A Twentieth Century Christmas Eve

The crowd was rushing to and fro,
    Last minute shopping must be done;
The time was short—'twas Christmas eve,
    There must be gifts for everyone.

A festive spirit filled the air
    And faces were aglow,
Despite the weary, aching feet
    That trudged through drifting snow.

A Stranger suddenly appeared,
    His whereabouts unknown;
No one seemed to know or care
    That He stood so alone.

Amid the busy, bustling throng,
    Apart He seemed to stand;
And as He watched the crowd surge by
    He beckoned to a man.

Said He, "Would you please be so kind
  To tell me what goes on?
There must be something special here
  To captivate this throng."

"My friend", said he, "do you not know
  This is the Christmas season?
We all give gifts and have a ball
  And never stop to reason."

The Stranger looked and saw a child
  Whose eyes lit up as she beheld
A doll so lovely in a store—
  It seemed to cast a magic spell.

Said He, "My dear, you seem so gay,
  Why are your eyes so bright?"
Said she, "Kind sir, do you not know
  That Santa comes tonight?"

The Stranger sadly turned away—
  Then—there before His eyes
Stood a little old lady, calm and still
  And looking very wise.

To the little old lady, the Stranger said,
  " 'Tis Christmas, so they say;
And what does Christmas mean to you,
  Is it just another day?"

"Oh, no!," the little old lady replied,
  " 'Tis not just another day,
Almost two thousand years ago
  Our Saviour came this way."

"He was born in a lowly manger
  In a stable in Bethlehem,
He came to save this sinful world,
  All who'd believe on Him."

The Stranger smiled, with eyes so kind,
  Yet sad, as He watched the throng
Pushing, shoving, for that one last gift;
  Then suddenly, He was gone.

                                    Louise Stroud

Christmas Message 1979

This Christmas as our thoughts turn to gifts and giving let us reflect upon God's gift to all mankind when, almost twenty centuries ago, a virgin brought forth a son—the Saviour of mankind.

Jesus Christ is the greatest Gift and the perfect Truth given to man.

The real value of the Gift and the Truth that IS Jesus Christ in the heart of man can best be judged by the calamities that must ensure when falsehood and imitation are substituted in His place.

The absence of Jesus Christ from the heart has led man to forge death-voiced weapons of war, pit brother against brother on the fields of civil discord, desolate the home, defile the church, choke noble channels of commerce, contaminate innocense, poison kindness, pollute the mind, murder love, desecrate the divine institution of marriage and much of what we hold sacred.

Earth can only offer death, disease and decay. But go to Bethlehem's stable, keep with Christ, follow Him to calvary's cross, put your hand trustingly in His, and though temptation, suffering and sacrifice await you, triumph will be yours at last.

Derek deCambra

There Was A Child

THERE WAS A CHILD
A Child so small that they laid Him in a manger
The night was still and calm, and the Child slept.
Upon His face was a smile—a smile of peace,
For the hay was soft and warm, and His mother was near.

THERE WAS A CHILD
A Child so filled with love that His glory brightened
    the heavens and settled upon a star.
The star shone.
The night was still and bright, and the Child slept,
Upon His face was a smile—a smile of love,
For He was the Child of God, and His father was near.

THERE WAS A CHILD
And once again we re-tell the story of the wonder of
    His birth.
But where is the manger?
Where is the still peaceful night?
Where is the love that so filled the hearts of men
    that the angels sang?
And how near—how near is the father?

THERE WAS A CHILD
And today He still lives. So come, let us go
Let us find the manger
Let us once more seek the still peaceful night.
Let us follow the star and worship Him.
Let us fill our hearts with His love,
Let us love one another.

Marian Heck

GOLDEN SCRIPTURE

And she brought forth her first-born son, and
wrapped him in swaddling clothes, and laid him
in a manger, because there was no room for them
in the inn.

Luke 2: 7

The Bus Token

Jenny stared unseeingly at the bright Christmas display in the store window. Crowds of hurrying shoppers surged around her but she did not see or hear them. Her mind was awhirl with disturbing thoughts. Why couldn't her parents understand even her most simple wish? Why couldn't she have been an only child without the handicap of three younger brothers? Surely a teen-age daughter should count for something. But, no, the entire family picked on her.

I get good grades in school, she thought rebelliously. *Better than Jim and John and Jerry. And I keep my own room neat—well, almost. I help with the dishes and baby-sit sometimes. Why can't I have that watch?*

With tightened lips she remembered her mother's words.

"Jenny, you have a watch and I see no reason to get you another. We have the boys to think of, too. We simply cannot manage to pay almost a hundred dollars for something you think you want."

"But, Mom, I'm not asking for anything else for Christmas. Just this watch. It's beautiful, Mom. The bracelet is really neat. No one else at school has one and I could be the first. Besides, it's practical. You can't tell it's a watch until you press a button and the time shows. It tells the month and the day, too."

"No, Jenny," her mother had said with unexpected firmness. "There will be no watch for Christmas."

Jenny turned from the bright lights of the store window and buttoned her coat. She wished the bus would come. She was wasting her time here but a store window was better than listening to her mother's unreasonable scolding. But she ought to get home and start on her lessons.

A small boy with a gray stocking cap pushed by her. He exclaimed in a shrill voice, "Look, Ma. There's the car I want. Do you think I could have that car for Christmas?" He pointed a grubby finger at the toy in the window.

Jenny looked down at the child, then at the toy which had prompted his excitement. She saw a tiny, inexpensive red automobile with rubber wheels and shining fenders.

The mother's voice was soft and tired. "But, son, it costs fifty-nine cents!" She spoke as if the amount were an absolute impossibility.

I wish I could get him the car, Jenny thought. *Poor little kid. He looks as if he has no toys.*

The boy continued staring at the bright red car, nose pressed against the window. He stood close to Jenny and she resisted an impulse to smooth his jacket collar.

Her fingers tightened around her small purse. *Why can't I give him the car?* she asked herself. *I've probably got the money with me now.* Almost reluctantly she counted her coins.

Four dimes, three pennies, and a bus token. Forty-three cents was not enough. She was surprised at her disappointment. *Let's see: the car costs fifty-nine cents and the tax would make it sixty-two. I need nineteen more cents,* she calculated quickly.

The bus token! But she would have to walk home in the cold and wind. It would be a long walk. Her hesitation was brief.

She separated the token from the dimes and pennies. Holding it between two fingers as if it were treasure, she walked into the store.

"Hello, Jenny," the man behind the counter hailed her. "Something I can do for you today?"

"Mr. Grimes, how much will you give me for this bus token?" She held it out.

"A bus token, huh? Well, I'll tell you, Jenny. I need to get home tonight and I go by bus." He laughed at his own little joke.

"I'll sell it to you, Mr. Grimes."

"The regular fare is twenty-five cents. I'll give you twenty cents for the token."

"I'll take it," she said and he handed her two dimes. She turned to see if the little boy and his mother were still there, his button nose pressed against the window. His eyes caressed the toy which could never be his.

"Mr. Grimes," she said hurriedly, "I want to buy a car like the one in the window for fifty-nine cents. I'm in a hurry."

"Okay, Jenny." He brought out a little box which he opened. "Is this the one?"

She nodded.

"You don't usually do your Christmas shopping here, do you? That will be sixty-two cents counting the tax."

She handed him the two dimes he had exchanged for the bus token. Added to them were her own four dimes and two pennies.

"Thank you, Mr. Grimes. 'Bye." Clutching the packaged toy, she almost ran from the store.

The woman and the boy were turning slowly to leave. He cast a last longing look at the toy in the window.

"Wait, wait!" called Jenny. They stopped uncertainly as she approached them.

"Here," Jenny said breathlessly as she thrust her purchase into the boy's chilled hands. "A Christmas present, for you." She turned and hurried around the corner.

The walk home seemed but a short distance to Jenny. She

Continued on page 154

Continued from page 153

breathed the cold crisp air in hungry lungfuls. She carefully read the faces of passersby—something she had never done. She found herself wondering about their homes, family circumstances, their joys and sorrows. She thought about the child with the new toy. *First time I've ever done anything for anyone outside of my family,* she told herself. She wondered at the strange exhilaration she felt. It was as if she were newborn.

When she reached home, she found herself running up the front steps with unaccustomed gladness. Her mother, dusting furniture in the hall, turned at her entrance.

"Hi, Mom," said Jenny. "I walked home. Had some thinking to do."

She noted her mother's pleased surprise when she took the dust cloth from her hands. Jenny began polishing an invisible spot on a small table."

"Mom, I've decided something," she said. "I don't want that watch after all. I don't need it."

Smiling at her mother's obvious relief, she added thoughtfully, "I've already had my Christmas."

Leland Mayberry

GOldEN pRAYER

Come, O Thou Prince of Peace, enter my heart and quiet all these wild alarms. Pour into my soul the Christmas message. Let me hear the anthem as it spreads over all the earth, and let me help the music onward, till the day when the universe will echo my heart's song, which echoes the angels' carol, which echoes Thy decree: Peace on the earth! Amen, blessed Christ.

Floyd W. Tomkins

Years That Used To Be

The shining, sparkling ornaments
Strung on our Christmas tree,
Reach out and take me by the hand
To years that used to be:

I am a little girl once more
Our tree wears candlelights,
We sing the songs the angels sang
And thrill to simple sights:

A star tops our small Christmas tree,
Red apples hug each bough,
Long strings of popcorn and bright chains
(If those days were here now!).

Gramp tells us of the Three Wise Men
Who came to Bethlehem,
I dream a little girlish dream
In which I follow them.

The shining, sparkling ornaments
Strung on our Christmas tree,
Reach out and take me by the hand
To years that used to be!

Annette Victorin

Vigil Of Christmas

Let no step fall,
Break no twig,
This is a night
Too big, too big
For sound at all.

Whisper no word,
Sing no note,
Let no bell ring
And no sound float
From man or bird.

Silence on earth
Is holy this night
As the old world dies
To a flicker of light
Before the birth

Of the new young King—
Silence for His cry
In a world so strange,
And the lullaby
His Mother will sing.

Anne Tansey

Family Album Favorite

O Little Town Of Bethlehem

When Phillips Brooks was rector of the Holy Trinity Episcopal Church in Philadelphia, he was asked to write a special song for the Sunday school Christmas celebration. "What shall I write?" he wondered, "How can I challenge the hearts and minds of our Sunday school with regard to Christ's birth—the place and manner of His birth, the reason for His birth, and the necessity of our new birth?" After much prayer, he felt that the Lord was bringing into focus an experience he had had a few years earlier in the Holy Land.

On Christmas Eve he had stood for a long time on a hillside and looked out over sleeping Bethlehem. In his imagination Brooks could see a weary couple making their way to the stable of an inn. There was no room for them in the guest section. He seemed to hear angel voices announcing to surprised shepherds, 'Behold, I bring you good tidings of great joy. For unto you is born this day, in the city of David, a Saviour, which is Christ the Lord.'

"How sad," he thought, "that in the inn there was no room for the One of Whom the angels sang—no room for the Son of God Who—though He was rich—yet for man's sake became poor, that through His poverty we might be made rich. But conditions have not changed; men still reject this One Who willingly took upon Himself the form of man in order to pay the penalty of the sin of man." From this reverie, Brooks turned to go to a midnight service to which he was pledged, and prayed, "O Holy Child of Bethlehem/Descend to us, we pray/Cast out our sin, and enter in/Be born in us today."

Brooks put his thoughts into verse, and when he had finished, he went to Lewis H. Redner, the organist and Sunday school superintendent, and said, "If you will write a suitable tune for these words, I will name it for you." On Christmas Eve the tune still had not come to Redner. Somewhat discouraged, he went to bed; and, as he slept, he dreamed he heard angels singing. He awoke, took up pen and paper, and set down the melody he felt was a gift from Heaven.

O little town of Bethlehem,
How still we see thee lie!
Above thy deep and dreamless sleep
The silent stars go by.

Yet in thy dark streets shineth
The everlasting light;
The hopes and fears of all the years
Are met in thee tonight.

Phillips Brooks, 1835-1893

First Snow

Whirling, swirling, tumbling down
First snow of Winter comes to town.
It changes trees to fairy queens
And sugar-coats the browns and greens
Of bush and shrub, of lawn and tree.
How white, how light
first snow can be!

Jean Conder Soule

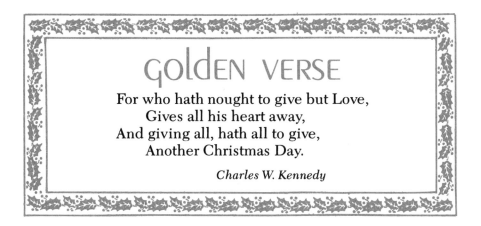

GOLDEN VERSE

For who hath nought to give but Love,
Gives all his heart away,
And giving all, hath all to give,
Another Christmas Day.

Charles W. Kennedy

Afterglow

The stable is quiet now;
If only those time-worn stalls could speak
what stories would be told!
They could tell of the lowing of the cattle,
the happy gurgling of a Baby;
or perhaps recall the awesome whispers,
the reverent prayers.
Would they relate the all-enfolding silence
as the star shone down?
Might they recount the hushed, though hurried plans
of a journey?
Alas, neither walls nor stalls can speak!
But that was yesterday,
and now,
the stable is quiet.

Gladys M. Seiders

City Robin

Rudy Robin cocked his ear
And said, "I'll not fly south this year.
This city park's just right for me.
There're lots of folks for company.
Plus tasty insects, bugs, and grubs.
Cherry trees, and berry shrubs.
So I won't join the bird migration.
I'll just stay here for my vacation."

So Rudy stayed through gray November;
Then came windy cold December.
The bugs were gone. The trees were bare.
And visitors were very rare.
Poor Rudy pecked the frozen ground
For scattered seeds that might be found.
His wind-chilled wings began to ache.
He feared he'd made a sad mistake.

"Perhaps," he sighed, "I should depart.
Yet, I'm a city bird at heart.
I like this place, indeed I do.
I'd love to stay the winter through."

One day a man named Mr. Draper,
A writer for the daily paper,
Spied Rudy pecking and a-bobbin'.
He cried, "My goodness! There's a robin!
One rarely sees a robin here,
This snowy, wintry time of year!"

The smart reporter did his duty.
He snapped a photograph of Rudy,
Who chirped at him and cocked his head.
That night the paper's headlines read:
THOUGH THE WEATHER'S COLD AND STARK,
A ROBIN WINTERS IN THE PARK!
To Ruby Robin's great delight,
He grew quite famous overnight!

The *Daily News* now spread the word.
So people came to see the bird
That dearly loved their city so,
He'd braved the ice and wintry snow.
They brought him pears and grapes to eat,
Some wool to warm his wings and feet.
And then a boy named Tim O'Toole
Brought a house he'd made in school—
A birdhouse, snug as it could be.
Tim set it in a maple tree.

Rudy now was there to stay;
No need for him to fly away.
People talked of him with pride.
Each day they came from far and wide
To see their little feathered guest,
Who dared to differ from the rest!

Frances B. Watts

Shepherd Boy

When angels gave the shepherds
Their tidings of great joy,
Do you s'pose that, among the men,
There was a shepherd boy?

And do you think he said to them,
"Oh, sirs, will you take me,
When you go down to Bethlehem,
The blessed Babe to see?"

And when they reached the manger,
Did he kneel in the hay
As close as he could get to where
The Baby Jesus lay?

And did he whisper softly,
"You are my Lord, I know;
When we grow up, I'll follow you
Wherever you may go."

Beulah H. Ragland

Caring For Him

When Baby Jesus Came to earth
Upon that cold, still night,
The stars shown down their very best
To give Him twinkling light.

The downy sheep crept close around
To keep the Baby warm;
The oxen stood with pointed horns
Protecting Him from harm.

The very straw lay softer
Beneath that Baby head—
I wish I could have picked Him up
And tucked Him in *my* bed!

Beulah H. Ragland

Winter Wonderland

This winter wonderland is mine,
To see and share with you.
Another gift of perfect love,
Another dream come true.

This winter wonderland is formed,
With jewels that shine so bright.
Each snow star has its own design,
Each crystal has its light.

This winter wonderland is filled
With trees that wear a gown,
Made out of dainty webs of snow,
With diamonds on each crown.

This winter wonderland is blessed,
With love that never dies,
Hand-crafted by the King of Kings,
Who made the earth and skies.

Patricia Ann Emme

Heaven

Come unto me, all ye that labor and are heavy laden, and I will give you rest.

Matthew 11:28

The Prodigal Son

With riches and youth to squander
The pleasure-bent *"prodigal son"*
Left the house of his Father
In search of adventure and fun—
And in reckless and riotous living
He wasted his youth and his gold,
And stripped of his earthly possessions
He was hungry and friendless and cold—
And thus he returned to his Father
Who met him with arms open wide
And cried, "My son, you are welcome
And a banquet awaits you inside" . . .
Now this story is told to remind us
Not so much of the wandering son
But *the unchanging love of the Father*
Who gladly forgave all he'd done—
And the message contained in this story
Is a powerful, wonderful one,
For it shows *our Father in Heaven*
Waits to welcome each *prodigal son*–
And whatever have been our transgressions,
God is waiting to welcome us back
And restore us our place in His Kingdom
And give us the joy that we lack . . .
So wander no longer in darkness,
Let not your return be delayed,
For the door to God is wide open
To welcome "the sheep that have strayed."

Helen Steiner Rice

The Departed

What are they seeking who are gone
Beyond our darkness to the dawn?
What are they doing who have left
Our world and us forlorn, bereft?
We cannot tell, we only know
That all untouched by pain and woe,
They are with Christ, oh, blessed rest!
What fairer lot, what life more blest,
Would we have chosen, if we could,
From all most fair and all most good?
They are with Christ; they see His face,
They know the fullness of His grace,
And they are learning, bright and clear,
The truth we only grope for here.

But how do we our time employ?
In mourning for our vanished joy?
Or are we growing, day by day,
In grace and wisdom, as are they?
Shall we be worthy of their love
When we shall meet once more, above?
Will mind and heart be tuned to share
These pleasures pure, that finer air?
Let us forget the little while
Ere we shall see their welcome smile;
Let us press onward, eager, bold,
Until Christ's face we shall behold,
And strive to make our lives more meet
To fall adoring at His feet.

Annie Johnson Flint

GOLDEN THOUGHT

Just over the hill is a beautiful valley, but
you must climb the hill to see it.

Author Unknown

I Don't Hear As Well As I Used To

I don't hear as well as I used to, God.
People have to shout and repeat things.
Frankly, a lot of what they have to say
Isn't worth repeating,
And the world's too noisy anyway.
The important thing is, I can hear,
Not with my ears, but with my heart,
What I really want to:
The children, when they were little,
Saying, "I love you, Mama."
Dan, when we lost all our savings,
Saying, "Hold me, Anne."
Stephen, in front of all those people,
Saying, "My mother should be
      receiving this honor
Instead of me."
My father-in-law, dying,
      laying his hand on my hair,
"You're a good girl, Anne. Carry on!"
It's no fun going deaf,
But there are worse things,
And I do have a lot of good memories
To listen to.

Elise Maclay

Aspiration

I wonder if the human touch, which people have, is not one of the greatest assets that you can have. You meet some people, and immediately you feel their warmth of mind or heart. You read a book, sit before the performance of a fine actor, or read a poem—and there it is—something that streams into your consciousness . . . Those who keep climbing higher, in their chosen work, all have this outstanding something. The nurse in the hospital, the man who delivers your mail, the clerk behind many a store counter, and the effective minister or public speaker. Without this human touch, hope has little on which to feed or thrive.

George Matthew Adams

Footprints In The Sand

One night I had a dream—I dreamed I was walking along the beach with the Lord and across the sky flashed scenes from my life. For each scene I noticed two sets of footprints in the sand, one belonged to me and the other to the Lord. When the last scene of my life flashed before us, I looked back at the footprints in the sand. I noticed that many times along the path of my life there was only one set of footprints. I also noticed that it happened at the very lowest and saddest times in my life. This really bothered me and I questioned the Lord about it.

"Lord, you said that once I decided to follow You, You would walk with me all the way. But I have noticed that during the most troublesome times in my life there is only one set of footprints. I don't understand why in times when I need You most, You should leave me."

The Lord replied, "My precious, precious child, I love you and I would never, never leave you during your times of trials and suffering. When you see only one set of footprints, it was then I carried you."

Author Unknown

The Reality Of A Dream

Let us wander away, you and I,
When darkness has covered the land
Help me count the stars in the sky
While holding my hand in your hand.

Let us rest on the beach, you and I,
Hear the waters washing the sand
Help me count the years that went by
The years that must finally end . . .

Let us live our love once again
With the sand, and the stars, and the sea
All the years of sadness and pain
Fade to nothing when you are with me.

Then, defying both time and tide
In the light of the stars by the sea
My shining, my beautiful bride
Will walk once again with me!

A. V. Riasanovsky

Shifting Sand...Seas...Seasons

I breathe deeply of the wondrous sea, awakened by the magic of spring. Noisy gulls flap wildly over the water, rippling in ribbons of pale sunlight. Birds, in formation, head northward against pink skies. White grains of sand, like precious moments of life, filter through my fingers. The air tingles with expectancy. It is a time for birth, rebirth and new beginnings . . . the promise of hope for

Summer peace. Blue skies are reflected in a joyous sea of changing hues. I smile under a healing sun and sing to the tune of the playful wind carrying colorful Frisbees over racing whitecaps. Living is vibrant, yet lazy . . . the promise of hope for

Fall contemplation. Deep in conversation, a stooped couple walk their dog close to the snapping surf. A coast guard plane flies low and disappears around the empty shoreline. Gulls call an urgent meeting on cracked, mossy pier posts. Under hazy skies, birds, in formation, head southward. I quickly take my last swim, then hurry to the warmth of my robe. Life is rich with experience . . . the promise of hope for

Winter dreams. The angry sea freezes under winter's icy fingers. The biting wind sends sand stinging against my cheeks. Capped with ice, the pier posts send long shadows over a carpet of snow that once was white sand. The silence becomes ominous and I turn toward home.

Roslyn N. Wallis

Lord, Polish Me

I walked along a sandy beach
In the early morning light;
The air was crisp, the water calm,
The sea gulls soared in flight;
I drank in all the beauty,
The scene was pure delight.

I sat upon a fallen log
And said a little prayer
Of thanks to the Almighty God
Who made our world so fair,
Who gave us all these lovely things
To prove to us His care.

And then I noticed that the log
Had a silky, satin sheen,
Worn smooth by years of storms and tide,
Buffeted by things unseen,
Polished 'til it shone like crystal,
Not at all like it had been.

Lord, I pray that all my trials,
All my suffering, grief and pain,
May sand off my sinful edges
'Til Your righteousness I gain.
Lord, polish me until I, too,
Reflect Your beauty o'er again!

Betty Anderson

golden thought

When we get to the place where
there's nothing left but God, we find
that God is enough.

Author Unknown

Bequest

When I leave you, there won't be
A million dollar legacy,
But I'll bequeath you something more:
Tender memories by the score
Of apple blossoms, wet with dew,
The thrilling moment when we flew
A paper kite from the hilltop
And laughed so hard we couldn't stop;
Mornings when the dawn was bright,
And evenings bathed in pale moonlight,
Suppers (when the rent was due)
Of crusty bread and Irish stew;
Ocean breezes and golden sands
Sifted through our sunburned hands.
Hours of joy and sometimes pain,
Days of sunshine and of rain.
Yes, I shall leave these memories,
Dearer by far than legacies.
So when you grow old, remember me
And the golden days which used to be.

Mary Ellen Stelling

Beautiful Thoughts

I remember the beautiful things
My baby's smile, a yellow bird's wings
An evening star in a midnight sky—
Clouds in pale blue, drifting by.
A cardinal's song, a sunset's glow—
Cooling rain, soft winds that blow.
Beautiful thoughts to be with me
And take to the brink of Eternity.
When youth and love
Have passed me by,
Beautiful memories
Can never die.

Lucille Crumley

Family Album Favorite

Requiem

Under the wide and starry sky
Dig the grave and let me lie.
Glad did I live and gladly die,
    And I laid me down with a will.

This be the verse you grave for me:
Here he lies where he longed to be;
Home is the sailor, home from sea,
    And the hunter home from the hill.

Robert Louis Stevenson

The Sound Of The Sea

The sea awoke at midnight from its sleep,
And round the pebbly beaches far and wide
I heard the first wave of the rising tide
Rush onward with uninterrupted sweep;
A voice out of the silence of the deep,
A sound mysteriously multiplied
As of a cataract from the mountain's side,
Or roar of winds upon a wooded steep.
So comes to us at times, from the unknown
And inaccessible solitudes of being,
The rushing of the sea-tides of the soul;
And inspirations, that we deem our own,
Are some divine foreshadowing and foreseeing
Of things beyond our reason or control.

Henry Wadsworth Longfellow

Heaven On Earth

Heaven's not a fenced-off place
In some far distant sky,
Nor is Eternity consigned
To some sweet by-and-by.

Heaven lies in every
Ordinary, common day.
We make our own Eternal life
Each step along our way.

Eternal time is measured
By a common hourglass.
We glimpse a bit of Heaven
As hours and minutes pass.

We only need the eyes to see.
The heart to count its worth,
To make our own Eternity
A Heaven here on earth!

Helen Lowrie Marshall

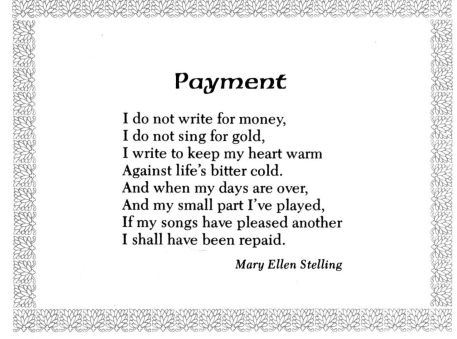

Payment

I do not write for money,
I do not sing for gold,
I write to keep my heart warm
Against life's bitter cold.
And when my days are over,
And my small part I've played,
If my songs have pleased another
I shall have been repaid.

Mary Ellen Stelling

The Answer

He was talking with his father
As most any boy will do,
Asking countless boyish questions
Ever old, yet ever new.

"I am growing, daddy, growing!
Will it always be this way,
And will God grow, just as I do,
Just a little bit each day?"

There's an answer to his question,
"Yes indeed, He surely will,
He will be your greatest comfort
As you climb Life's thorny hill!

"But no matter how you struggle
You will never understand
How the earth and starry heavens
Fit so nicely in His hand!

"Though you grow in mind and spirit,
Strength and wisdom till the end,
He will always be far greater
Than your mind can comprehend!"

Stillman J. Elwell

GOLDEN NUGGET

I find the greatest thing in this world not so much where we stand, as in what direction we are moving. To reach the port of heaven, we must sail sometimes with the wind, and sometimes against it, but we sail, and not drift, nor live at anchor.

Oliver Wendell Holmes

Immortality

Even now I sense
Beneath this cloak of flesh
God placed the fact
of everlastingness.

Deathless there burns
Within the human envelope
The light of life
The flame of hope.

John M. Drescher

Sundown

When my sun of life is low,
   When the dewy shadows creep,
Say for me before I go,
   "Now I lay me down to sleep."

I am at the journey's end,
   I have sown and I must reap;
There are no more ways to mend—
   Now I lay me down to sleep.

Nothing more to doubt or dare,
   Nothing more to give or keep:
Say for me the children's prayer,
   "Now I lay me down to sleep."

Who has learned along the way—
   Primrose path or stony steep—
More of wisdom than to say,
   "Now I lay me down to sleep"?

What have you more wise to tell
   When the shadows round me creep? . . .
All is over, all is well . . .
   Now I lay me down to sleep.

Bert Leston Taylor

Vision Through A Star

I gazed toward the purple horizon
    And into the night-realms afar,
Beheld in the distance arising
    Hope's beacon, the Evening Star.

Saw millions of others around it,
    All beaming with scintillant light,
But the Planet of Hope to my vision
    Was far more irradiantly bright.

It dazzled in shimmering glory,
    Five-pointed and laden with dreams,
The nebulous clouds floating near it,
    Reflecting the light in weird streams.

I saw the New World in my vision
    And gazed on the night-realms afar
While hope flamed anew in my bosom,
    Saluting the Evening Star.

Velta Myrle Allen

Sunset On The Lake

The breeze becomes a whisper,
Clouds seem to melt away,
The lake is getting ready
for the closing of the day,
Birches stand like sentinals
Along the green clad shore
Water rippled only by
A beaver's nightly chore,
Overhead, tree swallows glow
Like silver, darting by,
A lazy hawk glides motionless
Across the tinted sky,
Shadows fall on mountains, and
Gold edges show the sun
Is setting in full glory,
    Another day is done.

Edith Shubert

Falling Star

I saw a falling star
And ran and ran,
My hands outstretched and yet
I could not span
The bridge between its flash
And where I stood;
My aching hands were bare
My feet felt wood.

Oh, I have learned since then
A star can be
Reflected in a stream
That touches me.

Annette Victorin

Let's Read It Together
the children's corner

Give Thanks To God

In the beginning
   God made the world,
   Day was followed by night.
The sun ruled during the day,
   And the moon and stars
   Ruled at night.

God drew the waters
   From the land, the earth;
   And the waters He called the seas.
From the land He made
   Grasses and herbs to grow,
   And the flowers and the trees.

God made fishes and whales,
   Birds to fly,
   Beasts and creeping things.
He made them all
   For you and me;
   Thanks be to God for everything.

Edith G. Mize

ACKNOWLEDGMENTS continued from page IV

GOSPEL PUBLISHING HOUSE for "True Religion."

GOSPEL TRACT SOCIETY, INC. for "Jesus, It's Jim . . . Jim, It's Jesus," author unknown.

GUIDEPOSTS MAGAZINE for "The Dawn of Hope" by Ethel Rogers Mulvany, reprinted by permission from Guideposts Magazine. Copyright © 1962 by Guideposts Associates, Inc., Carmel, New York 10512.

HARCOURT BRACE JOVANOVICH, INC. for "Spring Grass" from *Good Morning, America*. Copyright © 1928, 1956 by Carl Sandburg. Reprinted by permission of Harcourt Brace Jovanovich, Inc.

HARPER & ROW, PUBLISHERS, INC., for "I Planted a Rose" from *Poems of Inspiration and Courage* by Grace Noll Crowell. Copyright © 1928, 1934 Harper & Row, Publishers, Inc., renewed 1956, 1962 by Grace Noll Crowell.

HAWTHORN BOOKS for "Sundown" by Bert Leston Taylor. Reprinted by permission of Hawthorn Books, Inc. from *One Thousand Inspirational Things*. Compiled by Audrey Stone Morris. Copyright © 1948. All rights reserved.

HOLT, RINEHART AND WINSTON for "A Prayer in Spring" by Robert Frost from *Poetry of Robert Frost* edited by Edward Connery Lathem. Copyright © 1934, 1969 Holt, Rinehart and Winston. Copyright © 1962 by Robert Frost. Reprinted by permission of Holt, Rinehart and Winston, Publishers.

HOPE PUBLISHING COMPANY for "A Wedding Prayer" by Margaret Clarkson.

IDEALS PUBLISHING COMPANY for "Happiness is as a butterfly, etc." by Nathaniel Hawthorne; "An open mind affords the opportunity, etc.," author unknown; "The Inscription at Mount Vernon," author unknown; "First in War, First in Peace" by Henry Lee; "Lincoln" by U. S. Grant.

JOHN KNOX PRESS for "Summer Rain" from *Thank You, Lord, For Little Things* by Annice Harris Brown. Copyright © 1973 John Knox Press. Used by permission of the publisher.

BOB JONES UNIVERSITY for "O Little Town of Bethlehem." Copyright © 1974 Bob Jones University, Greenville, South Carolina 29614. Reprinted from the November/December issue of *Faith For the Family*. Used by permission. All rights reserved.

McGRAW-HILL BOOK COMPANY for "I Don't Hear As Well As I Used To" from *Green Winter: Celebrations of Old Age by Elise Maclay*.

THE QUIET HOUR for "If I Had a Boy" and "The Link That Binds" by C. P. Bollman and "What Sort of Father Are You?" author unknown, from *The Quiet Hour Echoes*.

RANDOM HOUSE, INC. for "How the Pilgrims Built Their Towne in New England" from *The Landing of the Pilgrims* by James Daugherty.

READER'S DIGEST for "America's Folk Heroes" adapted from *The Story of America*. Copyright © 1975 by The Reader's Digest Association, Inc. Used by permission.

CHARLES SCRIBNER'S SONS for "Work" from *Music and Other Poems* by Henry Van Dyke. Copyright © 1904 Charles Scribner's Sons. Renewal Copyright © 1932 by Henry Van Dyke.

E. JACK SHARPE PUBLIC LIBRARY for "The Old Barn" by E. Jack Sharpe.

SIMON & SCHUSTER for "The Answer" from *Windows of Thought* by Stillman Ellwell. Copyright © 1971 by Stillman Ellwell. Reprinted by permission of Simon & Schuster, a division of Gulf & Western Corporation.

SUNSHINE MAGAZINE for "Holly in Your Heart," author unknown; "Just over the hill, etc.," author unknown; "The Hymn That Makes the Whole World Kin" by Vincent Edwards; "For who hath nought to give, etc.," by Charles W. Kennedy; "Love" by Dwight L. Moody; "He who allows a day to pass, etc.," by Lowell Thomas.

THE UNITED METHODIST PUBLISHING HOUSE for "Room to Spare" by Edith Mize. Copyright © 1977 by Graded Press.

WASHINGTON STAR SYNDICATE, INC. for "Aspiration" by George Matthew Adams from *The Editor's Scrapbook*, published by Ideals Publishing Company, Milwaukee, Wisconsin.

THE WESTMINSTER PRESS for "Something There Is About a Bird's Nest" from *It's Autumn*, text and photographs by Sister Noemi Weygant, O. S. B. Copyright © 1968, Sister Noemi Weygant, O. S. B., The Westminster Press. Used by permission.

WRITER'S DIGEST for "American Barns" by R. J. McGinnis.

ZONDERVAN PUBLISHING HOUSE for "Memories Are Not Forget-me-nots" by Clara Smith Reber from *Your Treasury of Inspiration* by Eleanor Doan.

WE ALSO WISH TO THANK

Velta Myrle Allen, Betty Anderson, C. P. Bollman, Geraldine Brook, Joan Beck, Barbara Dodge Borland for "A Boy and a Brook" and "October" by Hal Borland, Jamie Buckingham, Vicki H. Budge, Dorothy M. Cahoon, Leota Campbell, Ida M. Clark, Margaret Clarkson, Florence H. Cottrill, Lucille Crumley, Lois Mae Cuhel, Derek DeCambra, Esther Bird Doliber, John M. Drescher, Grace E. Easley, Stillman Ellwell, Patricia Ann Emme, Wanda Kirby Gardner, Dee Gaskin, Jaye Giammarino, Shannon Graham, Flora Allison Hagglund, Marian Heck, Esther B. Heins, E. Cole Ingle, Guye Johnson, Ruby A. Jones, Charles W. Kennedy, Nedra L. Krider, Rhena S. LaFever, R. D. Leonard, Jane Lindstrom, Amelia J. Locke, Linda Lowe, Lillus Mace, Mrs. Virgil Markham for "Lincoln, The Man of the People" by Edwin Markham, Clare Miseles, Edith G. Mize, Violet Munro, Winnifred Piper, Beulah H. Ragland, Ronald Reagan, A. V. Riasanovsky, Helen Steiner Rice, Vicki Lynne Sauers, Raymond Henry Schreiner, Garnett Ann Schultz, Gladys M. Seiders, Edith Shubert, Jean Conder Soule, Mary Ellen Stelling, Georgia May Stoddard, Louise Weibert Sutton, Alice MacKenzie Swaim, Louise Stroud, Anne Tansey, H. Ramsey Terhune, Shirley A. Thomas, Joseph D. Tonkin, Ethel P. Travis, Annette Victorin, Phyllis Walk, Nella Walker, William Arthur Ward, Frances B. Watts, Gwen Weising, Mrs. William Arnette Wofford for "Evening Worship" by William Arnette Wofford, B. L. Wolfe, Miriam Woolfolk, Dorothy Zimmerman.

WE ALSO WISH TO THANK

those contributors from whom we were unable to obtain a response prior to publication:

All Good Books, Eleanor DeGiulio, Geraldine Fay Gray, Adi-Kent Thomas Jeffry, Nick Kenny, Ann Landers, Dorothy Linney, Leland Mayberry, Jean Kyler McManus, Parent and Child Institute, Paulyne M. Penrod, Doris Philbrick, Solveig Paulson Russell, Perry Tanksley, Ruth S. Tomszak.

We also wish to thank Rita L. Moroney, Lucille C. Reading and Geraldine Zisk who were extremely helpful in obtaining permissions.

Type set by John C. Meyer & Son, Inc. Book printed and bound by R. R. Donnelley & Sons Company. Typography, design, layout and illustrations by Joseph V. Gorman. Pictures on pages 18, 35, 161 courtesy Camerique Photography; page 89 courtesy Harold Davis; pages 53, 179 courtesy Freelance Photographers Guild; pages 17, 71, 180 courtesy H. Armstrong Roberts; pages 36, 125, 143, 144 courtesy Shostal Associates; pages 54, 72, 90, 107, 108, 126 courtesy Fred Sieb; page 162 courtesy Vernon Sigl.

Diligent effort has been made to locate and secure permission for the inclusion of all copyrighted material in this book. If any such acknowledgments have been inadvertently omitted, the compilers and publishers would appreciate receiving full information so that proper credit may be given in future editions.

In the 13 star edition of The Family Album, the poem "Heart Gifts" on page 118 was attributed to Helen Lowrie Marshall. The poem was written by Helen Steiner Rice.

Dear Friend,

   As I work on the Family Album for you each year . . . I always feel a wonderful sense of peace. There are so many beautiful pictures to choose from . . . and so many really inspiring poems and stories to read.

   And it makes me ponder, and consider how strange life can be today.

   Man can walk on the moon, split the atom, he can harness the sun to heat his home . . . and yet so frequently today, he cannot find peace in his own heart.

   Perhaps we try too hard. We look too far. We seek too deep. For all we really have to do is stretch out our hand . . . and accept the peace and love of Jesus Christ. The peace that "passeth all understanding."

   He's always there beside us . . . He's never far. You can see Him in every sunrise . . . every tree . . . in every child's shining face. And I can see Him in so many of these lovely photographs and poems.

   He waits only for us to say "I'm ready." For didn't He say to us so long ago . . . "these things I have spoken unto you that in Me you might have peace . . ."

   So as we share the pleasures of this fourteenth Family Album . . . won't you let me share something else with you, too. Let me share the peace that I've found in Jesus by sending me your name and address and "How to Find Peace with God" by Billy Graham will be in the mail to you . . . as a gift from Nancy and me.

   Now . . . may you enjoy each and every page of this Family Album as much as we have enjoyed putting it together for you.

   And God bless you in all the days ahead!

                    Sincerely,

                    Arthur S. DeMoss

                    Arthur S. DeMoss